Domenico Scarlatti

Ninety Sonatas in Three Volumes

VOLUME III

Edited and Annotated by
Eiji Hashimoto

Dover Publications, Inc.
Mineola, New York

Bibliographical Note

This Dover edition, first published in 2012, is a revised and updated edition of the
work originally published by Zen-On Music Co., Ltd., Tokyo, Japan, in 2002.

International Standard Book Number

ISBN-13: 978-0-486-48617-8
ISBN-10: 0-486-48617-6

Manufactured in the United States by LSC Communications
48617605   2019
www.doverpublications.com

CONTENTS

Sonata LXXX (K. 482), Venice XI, No. 29

Sonata LXXXIV (K. 504), Parma XIV, No. 21

Sonata LXXIX (K. 481), Vienna Two Q. 15114, No. 3

Sonata LXXIII (K. 386), Cambridge 12, No. 15

DOMENICO SCARLATTI
AND HIS KEYBOARD MUSIC

Giuseppe Domenico Scarlatti was born in Naples in 1685. His father, Pietro Alessandro (1660-1725), a well-known composer in Rome, had been appointed by the Spanish viceroy in 1684 to the position of *maestro di cappella* at his court in Naples, a city which was under Spanish rule at the time. Domenico, who later changed his name to the Spanish Domingo, was the sixth of ten children born to Alessandro and Vittoria Anzalone, but their first to be born in Naples.

Scarlatti excelled in music from his early years, and his exceptional keyboard virtuosity became widely known during his sojourns in Venice (1705-1709) and Rome (1709-1719). Charles Burney relates that Thomas Roseingrave, a keyboard player himself, was staggered by Scarlatti's brilliant performance,[1] and John Mainwaring describes a keyboard contest between Handel and Scarlatti in which the former is alleged to have prevailed on the organ while they were about equal on the harpsichord.[2]

Leaving Italy, Scarlatti went to Lisbon, Portugal, where he became *mestre de capela* and keyboard instructor to Princess Maria Barbara (1711-1758), daughter of King João V, and to Don Antonio, the king's younger brother. When the princess wed the Spanish Crown Prince Fernando in 1729, Scarlatti accompanied her to Spain and remained there in her service until his death in 1757. It was for Maria Barbara, who became Queen of Spain in 1746, that Scarlatti presumably wrote the majority of his sonatas.

The queen must also have been an extraordinary keyboard player, judging from the degree of technical dexterity that many of Scarlatti's sonatas require. She too devoted her life to music, especially in her later years, and she must have appreciated Scarlatti's dedication and his genius, as she paid his gambling debts, bestowed a generous pension on his young widow, and in her will, bequeathed her ring to the Scarlatti family.

Curiously, though, there are many gaps in what is known about Scarlatti's life, his creative activities, and his association with and influence on others. We are not even certain about his personality. We do not know why or how the autograph manuscripts of his sonatas have disappeared. Nor do we know when he wrote the majority of his sonatas. Most of the Venice and all of the Parma manuscripts, copied by anonymous hands, date from 1752 to 1757, and it is possible that Scarlatti's creative genius was in full swing during this period. On the other hand, the dates shown in the manuscripts could indicate merely when they were copied from the lost source or sources.

Most of Scarlatti's sonatas are of binary design, and both halves are of approximately the same length. Walter Gerstenberg classifies the sonatas in three groups: (1) monothematic—usually symmetrical, (2) polythematic—usually asymmetrical, and (3) close to the classical "sonata form" with the recapitulation corresponding only to the later portion of the first half.[3] Ralph Kirkpatrick's analysis shows a somewhat different approach.[4] He describes Scarlatti's sonatas as being of two types, and each type is further divided into two categories. The first type is the closed sonata, in which both halves begin with the same thematic material. Sonatas of this type are categorized a) symmetrical or b) asymmetrical, the latter containing an excursion (modulatory passages in the opening portion of the second half). The second type is the open sonata, in which each half begins with different thematic materials. These sonatas are either a) free—often with entirely new material or with new material mixed with what has been heard in the first half in the excursion, or b) concentrated—using material of the first half in the excursion. There are, however, some sonatas which do not fit into any category. Kirkpatrick classifies these as exceptional forms.[5]

As for pairing of the sonatas, which Kirkpatrick advocated, it is supported by William Newman,[6] but rejected by Hermann Keller[7] and Giorgio Pestelli,[8] while cautiously discussed by Malcolm Boyd[9] and Joel Sheveloff.[10] The fact that an overwhelming number of the sonatas in Venice I-XIII and the corresponding sonatas in Parma (also many in Münster) are arranged as pairs in the same or parallel keys (and the same pairs are almost always found in both manuscripts) certainly draws our attention and must be by more than casual design. Kirkpatrick cites K. 99-100, K. 347-348, K. 526-527, etc.,[11] to

---

[1] Charles Burney, *A General History of Music,* Vol. II (London, 1782).

[2] John Mainwaring, *Memoirs of the Life of the Late G. F. Handel* (London, 1760).

[3] Walter Gerstenberg, *Die Klavierkompositionen Domenico Scarlattis* (Regensburg, 1933).

[4] Ralph Kirkpatrick, *Domenico Scarlatti* (Princeton, 1953).

[5] Examples of these categories from the present edition are: K. 13, 163 (symmetrical closed sonatas); K. 27, 541 (asymmetrical closed sonatas); K. 56, 200 (free open sonatas); K. 223, 360 (concentrated open sonatas); and K. 227 (exceptional form).

[6] William Newman, *The Sonata in the Classical Era* (Chapel Hill, 1963).

[7] Hermann Keller, *Domenico Scarlatti, ein Meister des Klaviers* (Leipzig, 1957).

[8] Giorgio Pestelli, *Le sonate di Domenico Scarlatti: proposta di un ordinamento cronologico* (Turin, 1967).

[9] Malcolm Boyd, *Domenico Scarlatti, Master of Music* (New York, 1987).

[10] Joel Sheveloff, "The Keyboard Music of Domenico Scarlatti: A Reevaluation of the Present State of Knowledge in the Light of the Sources" (PhD dissertation, Brandeis University, 1970).

[11] The Venice manuscript (1749) has only one heading, "Sonata II", for both K. 99 and K. 100; and both Venice and Parma indicate at the end of Sonata K. 347 *Al Cader dell' ultimo termino di questa Sonata, atacca subbito la Seguente, Come avisa la Mano.* (Upon completion of the last ending of this sonata, go immediately to the next one, as the hand indicates.), followed by the drawing of a hand pointing to the next sonata. Furthermore, K. 526 in C minor has two flats for its key signature in both manuscripts, but they are cancelled by two naturals at the beginning of the following sonata, K. 527 in C major. These sonatas are included in my earlier 100-sonata edition, but a situation similar to that in K. 526 and 527 is found in K. 509 and 510 in this 90-sonata edition.

support his theory and counts roughly 200 pairs, plus some groups of three. Both he and Newman also point to the two-movement scheme in keyboard works by other Italian composers of the time as further proof of their theory. We can find examples of this in the works of Francesco Durante (1684-1755), Baldassare Galuppi (1706-1785), Domenico Paradies (or Paradisi 1707-1791) and Domenico Alberti (ca. 1710-1740), etc.

Objections to this idea stem from the inconsistency of Scarlatti's sonatas dated before 1749, which are mostly arranged singly in different keys from one to the next, and from the fact that most of the sonatas are identified individually with their own numbers in the sources. It is true that some sonatas are paired in one manuscript but not in others and that four or five sonatas in the same or parallel key may be lined up together in the manuscripts. The pairwise arrangement, therefore, was not a rule, but probably a practice which Scarlatti began to use more consistently from the time he wrote the sonatas in the K. 90s on. And of course, even in these, there are some exceptions.

Barry Ife and Roy Truby[12] explain that a new trend of arranging sonatas in pairs or groups by key developed in Spain starting around 1750, possibly because of the demand by audiences for longer and more substantial works. They list examples, including 30 sonatas by Vincente Rodríguez (d. 1760), 30 sonatas by Sebastián de Albero (1722-1756), and, of course, sonatas by Scarlatti. Antonio Soler (1729-1783) went even further to introduce multimovement forms in different keys. The question of whether such pairwise arrangement in the manuscripts was made by Scarlatti or by the copyists remains without proof. Nevertheless, the main manuscripts were produced in the Spanish court, and they were in the possession of the queen, whose keyboard tutor was none other than Scarlatti himself. It is therefore highly unlikely that Scarlatti was not involved in making the arrangement or that he was not aware of it.

In the present edition, the paired sonatas (or sometimes a set of three) are linked with braces in the Contents at the beginning of each volume.

---

[12] *Early Spanish Keyboard Music: An Anthology,* ed. Barry Ife and Roy Truby, Vol. III (Oxford University Press, 1986).

SOURCES

The sources consulted for making Volume I of the present edition, but not applicable to Volumes II and III, are not listed here.

EIGHTEENTH-CENTURY MANUSCRIPTS

A. Venice

Fifteen volumes, containing a total of 496 sonatas (a few appear in more than one Venice volume). All of oblong format (approximately 26 x 35 cm.), 4 systems (8 staves) per page, with treble clef on the top staff and bass on the bottom.

These volumes, in anonymous hands, were acquired by the Biblioteca Nazionale Marciana in Venice in 1835 (Mss. 9770-9784). Kirkpatrick speculates that they were brought to Bologna from Spain by Farinelli[1] upon his retirement from the Spanish court. They were dispersed after his death and eventually acquired by the Venice library.

Each volume from I-XIII contains 30 sonatas, with the exception of Venice X, which consists of 34 sonatas. There are several sonatas in Venice I and II that duplicate sonatas in Venice 1742 and 1749 (including **K. 98** and **129**[2]), but among the sonatas contained in Venice I-XIII, there is no duplication. The dates are always indicated as part of the volume title on the opening page, and frequently at the top of the thematic index pages at the end of each volume. They are as follows: I and II, 1752; III-VI, 1753; VII-IX, 1754; X, 1755; XI-XII, 1756; and XIII, 1757.

Like the Venice 1742 and 1749 volumes, these thirteen volumes are bound in beautiful red morocco with the combined coats of arms of Spain and Portugal tooled in gold. The vivid colors of the tempo indications, clefs, hand indications, etc. seen in the 1742 volume (and to a lesser extent in the 1749 one), however, are mostly replaced by black (or occasionally brown). The musical text of the thirteen volumes is thought to have been penned by the same hand, which is different from the hands of the earlier volumes. It exhibits clear and proficient calligraphy. There are no cross-outs, or obvious traces of revised notes, or smudges, which occur routinely in Münster, Vienna I, and Vienna II. As in the case of his published editions and some other manuscripts, notes above c' automatically go to the top staff and those lower than c' to the bottom, regardless of hand distribution. Page turns are easy and practical, almost always coinciding with double bars, even though this may cause highly congested text at times, as in the case of the latter half of **K. 221** (which squeezes over 100 bars into an open folio). Only a few sonatas, like **K. 162** and **296**, however, require six pages due to their unusual lengths.

The title of each volume is short, and all are similar, like:

Scarlatti. / Libro 2⁰ / Año de / 1752.

SCARLATTY. / Libro 5. / Año de 1753.

SCARLATTY, / Libro 8⁰ / Año de 1754.

Each sonata is numbered either as, for example, SONATA / XV (Roman numerals in Venice I) or as Sonata / 15 (Arabic numerals in other volumes), often with the decoration ⚶ above the title "Sonata" (but not in the later volumes).

Most double bars are :||: or :‖: for the conclusion of the first half, with the occasional appearance of *Volti* or *V.ti* or *Segue*. Upon turning the page, however, the beginning of the second half is just like the initial bar of other staves, with neither double bar nor dots. The conclusion of a sonata shows :‖: *no* , with or without *Fin*. Trills are indicated interchangeably with *tr* or ⌒, and appoggiaturas in small notes are of diverse values with no apparent reason for the differences. A convenient index, consisting of two or three bars of the opening motif of each sonata on one staff, appears at the end of each volume with a heading like "Indice delas Sonatas que tiene este Libro. 1753."

The Venice collection is one of the two most comprehensive and most important Scarlatti sources available today (the other one is the Parma collection). The two are quite similar in calligraphy and layout, but with some discrepancies. A comparison of them will be made following the description of the Parma volumes.

B. Parma

15 volumes, 463 sonatas. (No pieces are duplicated in Parma.) All in oblong folios approximately 24 x 31 cm., 4 systems (8 staves) per page. Normally treble clef on the top staff, bass on the bottom, but a few with soprano, alto, and tenor clefs (as in **K. 69** and 87*).

Another large collection in unknown hand(s), these volumes are now housed in the Biblioteca Palatina, Sezione Musicale, in Parma (AG 31406-31420). Each volume contains 30 sonatas (except Volume VII, which contains 31, and Volume XV, which has 42). Their dates, like in Venice, are shown as part of the volume title (but not invariably) and/or occasionally on the index pages. Volume I, however, shows no date anywhere. Since its content is nearly identical to that of Venice I (1752), it must have been copied in the same year. The dates on the other volumes are as follows: Volume II-V, 1752; VI-VIII, 1753; IX-XI, 1754; XII, 1755; XIII-XIV, 1756; and XV, 1757.

This set lacks colorful decorations. The titles of the individual volumes, as in Venice, are all quite simple. For example:

---

[1] Farinelli's true name was Carlo Broschi (1705-1782). He was a famous Italian *castrato*, active in the Spanish court.

[2] Kirkpatrick numbers in bold print are included in the present edition. Those with one asterisk are from my edition of 100 sonatas, and those with two asterisks are from Kirkpatrick's edition of 60 sonatas.

Libro 1º.

Scarlatti / Libro 2º / Año de 1752.

Libro 14 del / Señor Scarlatti. / Año de 1756.

⁓ prevails for trills, although *tr*, or a mixture of the two signs in the same sonata, is by no means uncommon. Appoggiaturas in small notation appear in diverse lengths, which often differ from those of corresponding appoggiaturas in Venice. *Volti* or *V.ti S.to* or *V.ti Presto* and *Fine* at their respective endings are only occasionally seen. :‖: for the first ending and :‖: *no* for the end of a sonata are the standard markings. Convenient page turns practically all correspond to those in the Venice collection. The left-hand part moving onto the top staff or the right shifting to the bottom, in order to accommodate a higher or lower register respectively, is just as common in this manuscript as it is in others. The right side of the concluding bar of 21 sonatas in Parma XV shows the initial *S*. (*SA.* in two additional sonatas). A musician who was in the Spanish court at the time and whose name fits the initials was Antonio Soler (1729-1783), but there is no proof that Soler actually copied these sonatas.[3] The thematic index at the end of each volume is similar to what is found in Venice, except for that of Parma I, which is shown on two staves and carries the heading "Indice delas Tocatas que tiene este Libro."

Comparison of the Venice and Parma manuscripts: The Parma collection was probably the model for Münster, which in turn was used for making Vienna One. This means that these secondary sources more likely agree with Parma than with Venice in details. Venice I (1752) and Parma I (presumably 1752), Venice XI-XII (1756) and Parma XIII-XIV (1756), and Venice XIII (1757) and Parma XV (1757) have the same dates, and the order of the sonatas in these volumes often matches (except for the last 12 sonatas in Parma XV, which do not appear in Venice XIII). Furthermore, Venice III (1753) consists of sonatas from Parma IV and V (both 1752), and Venice VII (1754) contains a few sonatas from Parma VIII (1753) but mostly from Parma IX (1754). Sheveloff's speculation that Venice was copied from Parma, therefore, is feasible,[4] although this premise does not answer such questions as why there are over a dozen more pairs in Parma than there are in Venice, why the order of the sonatas from the beginning to the end of each volume is not always the same in the two sources, and why a few sonatas like **K. 177, 178, 199,** and **200** from Venice II (1752) are not included in Parma II–V (1752), rather in Parma VI (1753). Accordingly, it seems more likely that the Venice

and Parma volumes were both copied separately from a single lost source (possibly Scarlatti's original).

Discrepancies between Venice and Parma are neither numerous nor drastic, which is quite remarkable, considering the fact that the same 440-odd sonatas appear in both sources. Nevertheless, minor discrepancies do occur, such as the absence of trill signs and appoggiaturas or the omission of accidentals in one or the other source and differences in the pitches and lengths of certain notes, in groupings of short notes (e.g., ♪ ♬♬ vs. ♪. ♬♬ or ♬ ♬ vs. ♬♬♪), and in the notation of certain rhythms. These are individually cited in the Notes on the Text of the Sonatas. Some of these discrepancies, like differences in pitch or where there is one bar too many or too few, are undoubtedly due to human error; but the variance in rhythm (♬♬ versus ♫♫), though only occasionally seen, is worth noting. Taking examples from the present edition, we find that in **K. 98**, Venice 1749 displays ♬♬ , but the Venice II version gives ♬♬ , while Parma has ♫♫ (inaccurate) or ♫♫ ; in **K. 163**, Venice shows ♬♬ compared to Parma's ♫♫ (sometimes illegible, also occasionally ♫♫); in **K. 206**, bar 35, Venice has ♬♬ , while Parma shows ♬♬ (but in the corresponding bar 88 in the second half, both sources present ♬♬ , and in other locations in this sonata where ♬♬ or ♬♬ appears, the two manuscripts agree; in **K. 344**, bar 68, the situation is reversed (Parma ♬♬³, Venice ♬♬³), but ♬♬³ is found in all other locations in both sources. Since such differences, found in Scarlatti's other sonatas as well,[5] have an immediate and strong impact on one's performance, they are too significant to ignore by simply attributing them to copying issues.

The best-known example of elongating the first of evenly written notes is, of course, the *lourer* (long-short) in the predominantly French practice of *notes inégales*, which applies to a pair of evenly written notes in stepwise motion. Although the rules governing the *lourer* are complex, the availability of abundant and detailed instructions on the subject makes it easy to comprehend the practice. In comparison, rhythmic alteration of triplets is much less frequently and less clearly defined.

Francisco Correa de Arauxo explains two ways of performing triplets: one is to play the three notes evenly as written, which is easier; the other is to play them unevenly by holding the first note longer than the ensuing two notes for liberty and gracefulness.[6] The latter practice was apparently common among the organists of the time, even though it was more difficult to play.[7] Robert Donington compares the score

---

[3] Another name with the same initials is Sebastián de Albero, but he died in 1756 and thus could not have done the copying in 1757. In *Early Spanish Keyboard Music*, Vol. III (Oxford, 1986), Barry Ife and Roy Truby compare the Parma manuscript of one of Scarlatti's sonatas and a manuscript copy of a sonata by Albero made by his copyist. Since the two manuscripts are strikingly similar to each other, Ife and Truby speculate that Parma (and Venice) were actually made by Albero's copyist.

[4] "The Keyboard Music of Domenico Scarlatti", Vol.1, Chap.1.

[5] An exceptionally extensive difference in the two types occurs in K. 454*, in which Venice gives ♬♬ (with the figure 3 above it only a few initial times) while Parma presents ♫♫ throughout the entire sonata.

[6] *Libro de tientos y discursos de musica práctica y theórica de órgano intitulado facultad orgánica* (Alcalá, 1626).

[7] Correa leaves the choice of the place and the degree of elongation up to the performer's taste.

and violin parts of an opera manuscript by an anonymous composer (c. 1700)[8] in which the score shows three notes of equal length while the violin parts often indicate Siciliana rhythm (♪. ♪♪).[9] The pros and cons of lengthening the first of the three evenly written notes are further but sketchily documented in discourses of the eighteenth century[10] and even the nineteenth century.[11] In any case, the rhythmic differences seen in Venice and Parma were probably caused by the impression of the scribe(s) upon hearing these pieces, although the differences in rhythm must have been so minute that either notation could have been warranted.

C. Münster

> 5 volumes, 352 sonatas, approximately 26 x 32 cm., 4-6 systems (8-12 staves) per page. Treble clef on the top staff, bass on the bottom, but occasionally other clefs are used, as in Parma.

These 5 volumes were copied by different scribes (at least a half dozen or even more) in Italy, perhaps in Rome, sometime in the late eighteenth century. They were owned by the Roman Abbate Fortunato Santini (1778-1862), who collected some five thousand manuscripts and printed editions. Most of them later went to the Bischöfliche Santini-Bibliothek in Münster (Handschriften 3964-3968). Unfortunately, some were destroyed during World War II.

Münster I contains 90 sonatas (K. 466-555, almost all in the order of the Kirkpatrick numbers); II, 60 sonatas (from the K. 350s-465, about half of the sonatas following the order of the Kirkpatrick numbers, though some are absent, and a few in the K. 200s are included); III, 70 sonatas (mostly in the K. 200s, 300s and early 400s); IV, 70 sonatas (in the K. 100s and 200s, etc.); and Münster V consists of 14 fascicles with a total of 62 sonatas altogether. Although these sonatas are also seen in the Venice and/or Parma manuscripts, three—Münster V, No. 22 (K. 147*) and Münster II, Nos. 51 and 52 (K. 452 and 453)—are found in no other sources. The order of the sonatas in the Münster volumes differs somewhat from that in Venice and Parma, but the pairs remain mostly intact. For example, Münster II starts out with K. 364* and 365* both in F Minor (labelled Nos. 1 and 2), followed by K. 326 and 327 in C Major

(Nos. 3 and 4), K. 354 and 355 in F Major (Nos. 5 and 6), etc. In Münster V, fascicle A begins with K. 378 and 379 in F Major (Nos. 1 and 1a), then K. 376 and 377 in B Minor (Nos. 2 and 2a), and K. 374 and 375 in G Major (Nos. 3 and 3a), etc.

The hands in the Münster volumes vary from adequate to could-be-better. Ink stains, ink impressions from the other side of the folio, and revised noteheads over previously written ones also make reading difficult. Each sonata has its own number, but several different numbers by different hands may appear. Trills are indicated as ⌐, ⌐, ⌐, or ⌐, and the lengths of appoggiaturas also vary, depending on which scribe happens to have written them. The absence and inconsistency of these ornaments are more noticeable than in Venice or Parma. When an accidental is considered no longer valid, Venice and Parma likely leave the note without cancelling the earlier alteration. Münster and Vienna I, on the other hand, tend to supply a cancelling accidental as a precaution, which seems unnecessary at times, but helps at other times (see Notes on the Text for **K. 158** bar 66, **K. 224** bar 36, **K. 303** bar 7, etc.) Double bars range from :||: to :||: to || (as in the *Essercizi*). *Segui* or *Segue* (at the end of the first half) and *Fine* (at the end of the sonata) are seen conspicuously in Münster I, but appear less in later volumes.

Each volume and some fascicles in Münster V bear the title:
> Sonate per Cembalo del Sig.r D. Domenico Scarlatti

or something similar to it,[12] sometimes in one line, other times in two or more lines.

Münster serves as a good reference when differences between Venice and Parma occur. Although Münster tends to follow Parma, discrepancies even between these two versions are by no means uncommon. At any rate, this manuscript adds valuable information on Scarlatti's works.

D. Vienna One

> Seven volumes (A-G), containing 318 sonatas, including 17 which are duplicated in different volumes, 3 by Alessandro Scarlatti and 1 by Roseingrave. Oblong folio (21 x 29 cm.). Vols. A-F, 4-5 systems (8-10 staves); Vol. G, 4-8 systems (8-16 staves). Treble clef on the top staff and bass

---

8   Donington makes reference to a source in Rome, Biblioteca Apostolica Vaticana.

9   *Baroque Music: Style and Performance* (New York, 1982).

10   Those who insist on playing the triplets evenly include L. Mozart (*Versuch einer gründlichen Violinschule*, Augsburg, 1756, Chap. VI, §2) and D. G. Türk (*Klavierschule*, Leipzig und Halle, 1789, Chap. I, §64, though he writes that the first note should receive a gentle stress), while J. J. Quantz (*Versuch einer Anweisung die Flöte traversiere zu spielen*, Berlin, 1752, Chap. XII, §10) suggests the possibility of the first note being held slightly. C. P. E. Bach (*Versuch über die wahre Art das Clavier zu spielen*, Berlin, 1753, Pt. I, Chap. III, §28) does not mention triplets specifically, but talks about prolonging certain notes for the sake of expressiveness.

11   David Fuller, in his article "The Performer as Composer," quotes from a story of how two of Frédéric F. Chopin's friends observed his playing: "....both Hallé and Meyerbeer remarked how mazurkas under the fingers of Chopin sounded quite strictly duple, though notated in triple metre, and how angry it made him to have this pointed out. He felt and understood the metre to be 3/4, and even if the first beat was as long as the other two put together, it was 'still *à trois quatre*!' as he is recorded to have almost yelled at Meyerbeer." (*Performance Practice*, ed. H. M. Brown and S. Sadie, New York, 1989, Pt. I, Chap. VI). Fuller lists the source of this story as J.-J. Eigeldinger, *Chopin vu par ses élèves* (Neuchâtel, 1970).

12   A couple of small fascicles (fascicles D and G) from Münster V have the title *Toccate* (or *Toccata*) *per Cembalo / del Sig.r D. Domenico Scarlatti*, instead of *Sonate...* The first piece in fascicle D is K. 141* (Longo 422). Alessandro Longo titles this piece "Toccata" in his edition of *Opere complete per clavicembalo di Domenico Scarlatti* (Milan, 1906).

clef on the bottom. Occasionally other clefs are used, corresponding to Parma (as in **K. 69**), but not to Cooke.

These volumes, which once belonged to Santini's collection, are now housed in the Bibliothek der Gesellschaft der Musikfreunde in Vienna (VII 28011). Several scribes worked on them, including Santini himself.[13] Most of the sonatas bear the clefs and necessary sharps or flats for the key signature only on the first system of the page (or the piece). For the remaining systems, the top and bottom staves are simply braced together. Johannes Brahms owned the manuscript at one point, and he added thematic indexes, corrections, and other markings.

The title page of Vienna One A reads:

Sonate / XXXXII / di / Domenico Scarlatti[14]

However, there are 49 sonatas altogether, as numbers I through V contain two sonatas each (thus I is K. 378-379 in F Major, II is K. 376-377 in B Minor, etc.), and VI has three sonatas (K. 285, 286, 265 all in the key of A). But the pairing of sonatas soon disappears, and each sonata is in a different key from the previous one.

Vienna One B bears the title:

Sonate 68 / di / Domenico Scarlatti

Most of these sonatas are in the K. 100s and 200s, and pairing is well preserved. Johannes Brahms changed the 68 to 60, as the original numbering skips here and there, and some pages are missing.

Vienna One C, with a similar title, contains 45 sonatas from K. 466 through K. 513 mostly in that order, which correspond for the most part to those in Venice XI (the second half) and Venice XII (or Münster I from the beginning to the midpoint).

Vienna One D has 40 sonatas, all from the K. 500s and mostly in the order of Parma XV.

Vienna One E consists of 47 sonatas; but the content jumps from one K. number to another, and the pairing is not always consistent.

Vienna One F contains 18 sonatas, mostly from the K. 400s, and their pairing is largely intact.

Vienna One G is completely different from the rest in format (more systems per page and comprising separate fascicles), and it is in a different hand. Curiously, the title page does not come until between sonatas LIII and LIV. It reads:

LXIX / Sonate / dal Sig: / Domenico Scarlatti / ed / Allesandro [sic] Scarlatti, / suo Fratello[15]

Underneath is the *Lettore* found in the *Essercizi*, and beneath that appears *a Madrid*. Among the 59 pieces,[16] one is the piece by Roseingrave, 3 are fugues by Alessandro Scarlatti, and 17

are duplicates. Vienna One G includes 12 sonatas of the Cooke edition (K. 31-42). The various other clefs present in Cooke, however, are not found here; instead, the bass clef may be used on the top staff or the treble clef on the bottom staff when necessary. Special ornamental signs in Cooke, such as ⩘ for the mordent and ⩙ for a trill with turned ending, are indicated here as ⤳ and ⤳ respectively. ⩙ in Cooke is copied here as ℈. In a few instances where no relation to Cooke is evident (e.g., **K. 206**), however, ⤴ (presumably a mordent) appears. Altogether nine pairs of sonatas are found in Vienna One G, but the pairing mostly does not correspond to that in Venice or Parma (Nos. 6 and 7 are K. 40 and 115* in C Minor, Nos. 37 and 38 are **K. 135** and 215** in E Major, etc.). Page turns in this volume are at times unmanageable by the performer himself.

Vienna One as a whole is not an example of beautiful penmanship. It lacks the clear and tidy calligraphy demonstrated in Venice and Parma and is marred by miscopying, omissions, and revisions. Sheveloff claims that most of the sonatas in this collection were copied from Münster over a period of time, and this seems a logical assumption.

E. Vienna Two

179 sonatas (or 98 if duplicates are not counted) in 11 volumes of various oblong sizes. Mostly 4-5 systems (8-10 staves) per page. Treble clef on the top staff, bass clef on the bottom, but the use of other clefs is seen in a few sonatas.

In 1971, the Austrian scholar Eva Badura-Skoda discovered this previously unnoticed manuscript copy of Scarlatti's sonatas in the Bibliothek der Gesellschaft der Musikfreunde in Vienna (Q. 15112-20, Q. 11432, and Q. 15126). The sonatas were copied by various scribes.

Seunghyun Choi, who made a subsequent study of the manuscript,[17] speculates that some sonatas were copied in the 1750s and 1760s, but most of them between 1770 and 1790. They were acquired by a Viennese diplomat and music lover, Adeodatas J. P. du Beyne de Malchamps (1717-1803), alias Joseph Du Beine. After his death they were auctioned, going to Beethoven's patron the Archduke Rudolph and eventually to the Bibliothek.

Q. 15112 and Q. 15113 together include all of the sonatas found in the *Essercizi*, except K. 30*. Q. 15112 has 6 (K. 8, 16**, 19, 9*, **27**, **14**, in this order), and Q. 15113 has the remaining 23 (in the same order as in the *Essercizi*). Q. 15114 has 16 sonatas, mostly in the late K. 400s, and Q. 15115, a

---

[13] Sheveloff speculates that A and E are by one scribe, while B, C, D, and F are by another, and G is by a third; but which one was copied by Santini is unclear.

[14] Another hand indicates "Johannes Brahms / fogli 19 ½" underneath.

[15] LXIX looks like different handwriting, and the "I" between the two "X"s seems like a smudge. There are only 59 pieces, not 69.

[16] Kirkpatrick's numbering of Vienna One G excludes Roseingrave's piece (No. 11) but includes Alessandro Scarlatti's fugues (Nos. 48, 49, 52). For the sake of consistency, I have included all of the pieces to make 59.

[17] "Newly Found Eighteenth Century Manuscripts of Domenico Scarlatti's Sonatas and Their Relationship to Other Eighteenth and Early Nineteenth Century Sources" (Phd dissertation, University of Wisconsin, 1974).

potpourri of 6 sonatas. Q. 15116 consists of 13 sonatas (K. 100s-200s), all of which are dated individually, mostly "Anno 1752".[18] Q. 15117 has 22 sonatas, including Roseingrave's piece and 3 fugues by Alessandro Scarlatti, the K. 8 variant, and K. 31-42, plus some extra sonatas, mostly in the K. 100s. Q. 15118 has 8 sonatas; Q. 15119, 10 sonatas; and Q. 15120, 3 sonatas.

There is yet another set, bound together. The cover leaf reads "Raccolta / di tutti Sonate / per il Clavicembalo / del Signore / Dominico SCARLATI."[19] The *Raccolta* (collection), Q. 11432, includes 72 sonatas in 12 fascicles, each containing 6 sonatas. Each fascicle has its own title: "Opera I.mo / 6 / Sonates Per il / Clavi Cembalo / Del Sig.e: Dominico Scarlati," "Opera II.do / 6 / Sonates Per il / Clavi Cembalo / Del Sig.e: Dominico Scarlati," etc. The pieces in fascicles I and II and the first three in fascicle III are the same sonatas, in the same order, as those found in Q. 15114. The sonatas in the remainder of fascicle III through fascicle VII duplicate those in Q. 15116, Q. 15115, and Q. 15118 in the same order, and those in fascicles VIII through XI are replicas of the sonatas in Q. 15112 and Q. 15113, but in random order. Fascicle XII contains mostly sonatas from Q. 15117 in the same order.

Choi suspects that the *Raccolta* was copied around 1780, later than the other Vienna Two volumes. The *Raccolta's* calligraphy is tidy and clear, but page turns are much less convenient than in other sources, and hand designations are spotty at best—in fact fascicles V and X omit practically all of them.

In general, the Vienna Two volumes do not show much attention to pairing of sonatas. There are only a handful which correspond to the pairs in Venice and Parma, and a few others in the same key but not matching those in Venice or Parma (e.g., Q. 15114, Nos. 8 and 9 are K. 450 and 426** in G Minor).

The provenance of Vienna Two seems varied. The *Essercizi* (or Witvogel) and Cooke (or one of its reprints) must have been used directly for Q. 15112, Q. 15113, and Q. 15117. The order of the sonatas in Q. 15113 and Q. 15117 corresponds to that in the *Essercizi* and Cooke respectively (that in Münster and Vienna One does not), Roseingrave's piece and the K. 8 variant are found in Q. 15117, and the mordent sign found in Cooke (not in Vienna One) is preserved here (though not always).[20] Q. 15116 was likely copied from Parma, while Q. 15114-15115, the rest of Q. 15117, and Q. 15118-15120 must have been extracted chiefly from Münster (which they resemble in details), as well as from Vienna One, Parma, and the Boivin edition. The *Raccolta* undoubtedly came from the earlier Vienna Two volumes.

F. Cambridge

Two volumes, containing 31 and 24 sonatas respectively. Fairly small, oblong shape (19 x 24 cm.). Mostly 4 systems (8 staves) per page. Treble clef on the top staff and bass clef on the bottom.

Lord Richard Fitzwilliam, an English music collector, went to Madrid in 1772 and acquired two manuscript volumes of Scarlatti's works. They are now in the Fitzwilliam Museum in Cambridge. The first volume (32 F 12) must have been copied by several scribes. The title page reads "Sonatta / Clavicordio / D.n Domingo / Escarlati." The sonatas included are mostly in the K. 400s and 500s, although a few in the 200s and 300s are mixed in, sometimes in pairs but other times not. The other volume (32 F 13) bears the title in ornate calligraphy: "Libro de Sonatas de / Clave Para el ex.mo s.or / Eñbaxador de. / Benecia. / De D.n Domingo Scarlatí.," suggesting that they were copied for the Venetian ambassador. The majority of the pieces are in the early K. 100s, plus a few early sonatas seen in the *Essercizi*. Only one scribe must have copied all the sonatas in this volume, which is quite neat and legible. In neither of the two volumes, however, were page turns taken into account. Owing to the generous spacing of notes, which results in fewer bars on a page, each half extends beyond an open folio. Yet the end of a half may come in the middle of a page, and then the next half or the following sonata begins on the system immediately below it. Two sonatas in Cambridge 13, Nos. 5a and 7a, do not exist in any other sources. Kirkpatrick numbers them K. 145 and 146.

---

[18] These dates are obviously those indicated in the Venice and/or Parma manuscripts.

[19] His name is misspelled throughout the *Raccolta*.

[20] Curiously, ⌁ , which resembles the sign for a mordent, appears in Q. 15116 (such as in **K. 135**, bar 18, and in **K. 206**, bars 19 and 66, in the present edition). It may have meant *t*, but interpreting it as a mordent is unsuitable. Another sign ∞ is also seen in Q. 11432, as in **K. 13**, **K. 27** (bars 7 and 9), **K. 135** (bar 18), etc.; but this seems to be a calligraphic variation of ⌂ . These ambiguous signs are mentioned individually in the Notes on the Text and also in Scarlatti's Ornaments and Their Performance in Volumes II and III.

EDITORIAL POLICY

Over thirty years have passed since my first urtext edition of sonatas by Domenico Scarlatti—100 sonatas in three volumes —was published, and ten years have elapsed since my subsequent edition of 90 sonatas originally came out. Recently, I decided to revise both sets, but to keep each set independent from the other rather than combining the sonatas sequentially in a single large collection. One will therefore notice some differences in editorial policy between the two sets.

The K. preceding the sonata numbers is the initial of Kirkpatrick, a well-known Scarlatti scholar who catalogued Scarlatti's keyboard works according to the chronological order of a few editions and the large volume of unpublished manuscripts from the eighteenth century. This is the order which I followed in compiling my two sets of Scarlatti's sonatas. Needless to say, none of the sonatas here duplicate those in my earlier edition of 100 or Kirkpatrick's edition of 60.

1. General Policy

All of the individual sources listed at the beginning of each sonata have been examined in making this edition. While it was not my intention to report every single difference revealed in them, discrepancies among the primary sources (namely the *Essercizi* edition, the Witvogel edition, and the Venice and Parma manuscripts) are carefully addressed in the Notes on the Text of the Sonatas at the end of each volume. As for the secondary sources (Cooke, Boivin, Münster, Worgan, Vienna One and Two, and Cambridge), remarks are made if deviations

from the primary sources are deemed significant (for example, when an accidental or notes absent in the primary sources are shown), or if differing versions from the primary sources are equally reasonable, sparking curiosity about other opinions, or if a secondary source is the only additional one available for consultation.

2. Original Presentation Preserved

(a) Sharps and flats in key signatures in the sources do not always conform to modern practice; there may be one less than expected (see **K. 20, 22, 43, 244, 245, 343, 344,** etc.). Unlike my policy in the 100 Sonatas, I copied them in the 90 Sonatas exactly as they appear in the sources, because this gives a better idea of what the scores show. When editorial accidentals would be helpful, I have added them above the notes (see **K. 20,** bars 41-46; **K. 47,** bar 63; etc.). Lest the reader be misled by the number of sharps or flats shown in the key signature, I have indicated the key of a sonata along with its Kirkpatrick number above the opening bars.

(b) Rests are commonly absent in the sources, and these spaces are left blank. I refrained from inserting rests in these places, unless the blank space makes the entrance of notes unclear.

(c) The beamings of eighth or sixteenth notes in the sources are preserved here, taking possible rhythmic implications into account. Exceptions, however, are when the sources show different beamings in identical or parallel passages (**Ex. 1a**), when lack of space prevented the use of normal beams (**Ex. 1b**), and/or when misleading beaming was found in the

Ex. 1a K. 13

Essercizi

Ex. 1a K. 242

Venice

Ex. 1b K. 20

Essercizi

Ex. 1b K. 242

Venice

Edited version

Ex. 1c K. 150

Venice

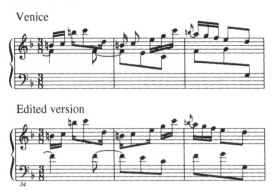

Edited version

✳ appoggiatura from Parma

See also Ex. 2a K. 47 bars 26-27.

sources (**Ex. 1c**). These have been amended as shown.

(d) Unless the sources show the numeral 3 above triplets, I did not indicate the 3. The musical context should be clear enough without the unnecessary addition.

(e) Though rhythmically inaccurate, notation like (**K. 1**, bar 12; **K. 124**, bars 33, 35, etc.) or ![notation] (**K. 50**, bars 136, 138, etc.) has been preserved.

3. Editorial Revisions

(a) The common practice of the time was that an accidental applied only to the note immediately following. This meant that an accidental had to be added each time the note was altered even within the same bar. Otherwise the note was understood to be governed by the key signature (**Ex. 2a**). When notes on the same pitch were reiterated without any interruptions, however, the power of one accidental carried

through all the way, even beyond the bar line (**Ex. 2b**). This was the basic practice, but of course there are a number of instances where accidentals were taken for granted or forgotten, and a cancelling sign (usually a natural, but sometimes a flat to cancel a sharp) is absent. I have revised the application of accidentals in accordance with modern practice (i.e., one accidental is applicable to the notes on that pitch thereafter until the end of that bar). Occasionally, however, I have added an accidental toward the end of the bar if there are so many chromatic alterations that the status of the notes toward the end becomes ambiguous, or if the original accidental has appeared too far back in the same bar. A list of added accidentals is given for each sonata in the Notes on the Text.

In the sources, a double sharp is sometimes indicated by an additional sharp where the key signature already indicates a

Ex. 2a K. 47

Venice

Edited version

Ex. 2a K. 200

Venice

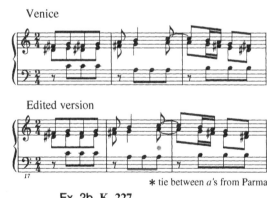

Edited version

✳ tie between *a*'s from Parma

Ex. 2b K. 206

Venice

Edited version

✳ appoggiatura from Parma

Ex. 2b K. 227

Venice

Edited version

sharp to make a total of two sharps (**K. 206** see Ex. 2b, **K. 371**, 531). At other times, the enharmonic pitch G♮ or D♮ instead of F✕ or C✕ may be seen (**K. 244, 245**). They have been replaced by the double-sharp sign ✕. Likewise, B♮ has been changed to C♭ (**K. 244**), when the context is appropriate.

(b) The sources mostly adhere to the practice of assigning the treble clef to the top staff and the bass clef to the bottom without taking proper hand distribution into account. When both hands are engaged in higher registers, therefore, the top staff displays all of the notes, while the bottom one is left empty. This has the advantage of not requiring many ledger lines or excessive changes of clefs. On the other hand, it often causes one staff to be extremely congested, making it difficult to sort out which hand should play which notes.

I kept the original arrangement in two-part textures (as the hand distribution is clear enough), or where there are numerous wide jumps back and forth by one hand in which frequent change of clefs would look cumbersome to the player, or in a continuing melodic line (**K. 223, 224**). Otherwise, I brought the treble clef to the bottom staff or the bass clef to the top as necessary to keep the notes for each hand on its own staff. Unless *M* and *D* indications appear in the sources, the assigning of various voices to each hand was done at my discretion.

While I retained the original manner of notation for hand crossings (**K. 27**), I sometimes introduced a third staff for clarity (**K. 47**).

(c) Stems in the sources are generally drawn separately for each single voice (as are their beams and flags), even in chordal texture. While this makes it easy to follow a linear line, reading can be extremely strenuous for the eyes (Ex. 1b, 2b **K. 206**). Binding all the voices of the same value with one stem would make it simpler; but then, although the vertical harmony would be well perceived, the subtle linear movements would be less recognizable. When there are two voices on a staff, therefore, I separated them using upward and downward stems. When there are three or more voices

on a staff, I customarily gave the outermost voice (soprano on the top staff, bass on the bottom staff) a separate stem, and combined the rest together (**K. 122**, bars 12-25).

(d) The hand designations *D (destra)* and *M (manca)* have been changed to *R (right)* and *L (left)* respectively. Tempo indications like *Allº* and *Andᵉ* have been spelled out in full. Certain notes have been presented differently in accordance with the time signature (**Ex. 3**). Such indications as *Volti, Vᵗⁱ Pᵗᵒ, Volti subito, Segue*, etc., at the end of the first half, and *Fin, Fine, D.C.*, etc., at the end of a sonata have been omitted, as their inconsistent presence and diverse vocabulary would invite unnecessary confusion. Triplets in the value of an eighth note, indicated as ♫, have been changed to ♫.

(e) The manuscript copies of Scarlatti's works frequently show large bowed lines, drawn over and under the notes, bridging the last bar of the first half and the beginning of the second half (see the facsimile of **K. 221** at the beginning of Volume II). In some cases, they are assumed to be [1.⌐ ⌐2.⌐ (**K. 12**, **K. 56**, **K. 206**, **K. 360**, etc.). But this assumption does not make sense in many other instances, because skipping the first ending and proceeding to the second half of the sonata would result in the leading tone being followed by a rest rather than its tonic note (**K. 386, 418, 484**, etc.). Considering the bowed lines as ties—if the notes in both bars are on the same pitch—is also impractical (**K. 343, 541**, etc.). Therefore, these bowed lines could, in some cases, simply be a reminder to turn the page quickly and continue the piece, or a notational habit of the scribe. Nevertheless, I have listed all these instances in the Notes on the Text, so that the reader may draw his own conclusions.

(f) Trills, appoggiaturas, accidentals, notes, and rests, etc. in parentheses are what appear in the secondary source or sources. Those in brackets are my editorial additions. ⌐ is an editorial slur or tie, and a small accidental above or below a note is also an editorial supplement.

Ex. 3 K. 135

Venice

Edited version

Ex. 3 K. 370

Venice

Edited version

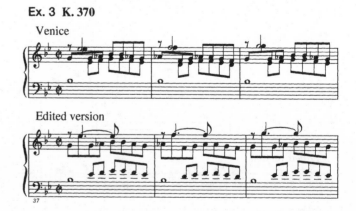

SCARLATTI'S ORNAMENTS AND THEIR PERFORMANCE
PART II

THE TRILL

The trill is one of a very few ornaments which have been indicated consistently by signs instead of actual notes. This is because trills require more notes than any other ornaments, and writing them in actual notes is difficult and inaccurate. Therefore, many composers of the seventeenth and eighteenth centuries made use of various trill signs, which unfortunately were not always the same from one composer to another.

Scarlatti's trills appear quite simply in the primary sources (the Venice and Parma manuscripts) as *tr* or ⌁.[1] The difference between these two signs, however, must be insignificant, as one manuscript may indicate *tr*, while another gives ⌁ in the same location in the same sonata; and even in one manuscript, there may be a mixture of the two signs in corresponding passages of the same sonata. These facts may give us the impression that Scarlatti's trills are easy to understand; yet this is far from true, because Scarlatti (and/or

his scribes) assigned more complex roles to these simple signs and probably assumed that the performers themselves would know the proper interpretation. French and German composers, on the other hand, used many diverse signs, such as ⌁ , ⌁ , ⌁ , ⌁ , and ⌁ , each applicable to a different context.

We shall now examine the actual meanings of Scarlatti's trill signs.

The assumption that Scarlatti's trills begin with the upper auxiliary note must be generally correct, as this was a common practice at the time,[2] and it makes sense in Scarlatti's works as well. But beyond this, there are many questions and ambiguities. For example:

(a) The upper appoggiatura appears inconsistently before trilled notes in the sources (**Ex. 1**). An appoggiatura might be seen where it would be clearly understood anyway (**Ex. 2a**); yet when its presence would be of help, it is often absent (**Ex. 2b**).[3] Incidentally, Ex. 2b demonstrates two different trill endings—**K. 302** with a two-note suffix, and K. 487* without it—even though they are in similar contexts.[4]

Ex. 1
K. 17   Presto

Essercizi, Witvogel

[Witvogel: trills *t*]

K. 159   All?

Venice, Parma

[Parma: appoggiaturas ♪]

Ex. 2a
K. 125   Vivo

Venice, Parma

[Parma: ⌁ over first *e* on bottom staff in bar 61]

K. 243   Allegro

Venice, Parma

Ex. 2b
K. 302   And?

Venice, Parma

K. 487*   Allegro

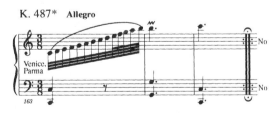

Venice, Parma

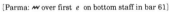

[1] The *Essercizi* edition gives the sign ⌁ , but the Witvogel edition replaces it with *t*. The secondary manuscripts, like Münster, Vienna I and II, etc., however, exhibit *tr*, ⌁, *t*, ⌄ , and ✛ .

[2] Many French and German treatises mention this, and a few Italians like Pier Francesco Tosi, in his *Opinioni de' cantori antichi, e moderni* (Bologna, 1723), Francesco Geminiani, *A Treatise of Good Taste in the Art of Musick* (London, 1749), and Nicolo Pasquali, *The Art of Fingering the Harpsichord* (Edinburgh, 1758) advocate starting the trill on the upper note.

[3] C. P. E. Bach says that the variable [long] appoggiatura is found before cadential trills (*Versuch*, Chap. II, Sec. ii, §9). L. Mozart expresses a similar opinion, saying that if the trill occurs in the middle of a passage [his example shows a cadential trill], the appoggiatura is held through half the value of the [trilled] note (*Violinschule*, Augsburg, Chap. X, §11).

[4] J. J. Quantz writes that the ending of each trill consists of two little notes. If a plain [trilled] note is found, both the appoggiatura and termination are implied (*Versuch einer Anweisung die Flöte traversiere zu spielen*, Chap. IX, §7). C. P. E. Bach explains that trills on notes of a certain length are played with a termination (*Versuch*, Chap. II, Sec. iii, §13).

(b) When trill signs are present over extremely short notes in a fast tempo, playing them as trills is virtually impossible (**Ex. 3a**). Could Scarlatti have meant them to be short appoggiaturas instead? **Ex. 3b** suggests this.[5]

(c) When a lower auxiliary note precedes a relatively long note with *w* or *tr*, interpreting them in combination as the ascending trill (without suffix) seems to be relevant (**Ex. 4a**). Occasionally, there might be three preceding notes instead of one (**Ex. 4b**), but both must signify the same thing. However, in **Ex. 4c**—similar to Ex. 4a, but in an ascending context where the ensuing note does NOT descend a second—the mordent is generally considered to be the appropriate ornament.[6] Taking *tr* or *w* as the mordent may seem out of the question, but Scarlatti never used the mordent sign; also, in a situation like K. 516** (Ex. 4c) with *w* over two notes in an octave span, playing a trill would be strenuous work, especially for those who have small hands. Interpreting *w* as a mordent instead might be worth considering.

Ex. 3a
K. 126*

[Venice: ♮ before *a′* in bar 97 missing
Parma: ♪ instead of ♪ in 97 and 99; trills *w*]

K. 383 Allegro

Ex. 3b
K. 129 Allegro

K. 271 Vivo

[Parma: trill *tr*]

Ex. 4a
K. 51 Allº

[Cambridge: no tempo indication; appoggiatura ♪ in (not before) 47, but no trill]

K. 106 Allº

[Parma: Andᵗᵉ; trill *w*]

K. 127* Allegro

[Parma: appoggiaturas in bar 14 ♪ and ♩ respectively; trill *w*]

Ex. 4b
K. 128* Allº

[Parma: trill *w*]

K. 260** Allº

---

[5] C. P. E. Bach: In very fast tempos, the effect of a trill can be achieved by the use of the appoggiatura (*Versuch*, Chap II, Sec. iii, §18).

[6] C. P. E. Bach says that the mordent is suitable in an ascending second (ibid., Chap. II, Sec. v, §14), whereas the short trill (see Ex. 7a) is better for a descending second (ibid., Chap. II, Sec. ii, §30). Türk is of the same opinion (*Klavierschule*, Chap. IV, §63).

Ex. 4c

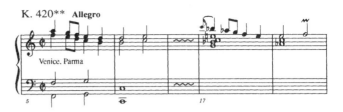

(d) **Ex. 5**, is a different case, however, and it should be interpreted as a regular trill without being influenced by the preceding note a step below. Because the two notes belong to different chords, they are not in the relation of an appoggiatura and the main note. Hence the trill has to start on the upper note to stress the second beat.

(e) When the trill follows a *ribattuta* (as its continuation)[7] (**Ex. 6**), the same type of oscillation should continue without interruption. Accordingly, it would be logical for the trill itself to maintain the main-note start.

Ex. 5

[Parma: appoggiatura ♪]

Ex. 6

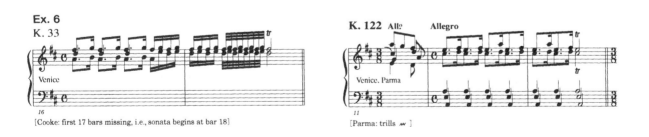

[Cooke: first 17 bars missing, i.e., sonata begins at bar 18]

[Parma: trills ⌅]

---

[7] A *ribattuta* is similar to a trill, but starting on the main note in dotted rhythm and accelerating. Monteverdi, Caccini, Tartini, and Vivaldi (in his *The Seasons*, Op. 8, No. 1, first movement) among others used it.

(f) The short trill (known as the half or compact trill) consists of three notes (the main, upper, and main notes), and it is appropriate in a descending line in a brisk tempo (**Ex. 7a**).[8] Whether Scarlatti used the short trill or not is uncertain, but in **Ex. 7b**, it would be more practical to use the short trill than the regular trill. The short appoggiatura, (shown in Ex. 3b), might be another option.

(g) When the trill sign is found in a quick ascending context (**Ex. 8**), interpreting it as the turn seems to be appropriate.[9]

The examples shown thus far demonstrate the complexity of interpreting Scarlatti's trills. Nonetheless, the players of the time, using the manuscript copies (or the early published editions), must have been accustomed to interpreting the simple signs properly and variously—a skill we lack.

What we need to do, then, is to acquire some information on eighteenth-century ornaments and to consider the possibilities according to the context. The present short article is only the beginning, but hopefully it demonstrates the possibility of interpreting the trills variably according to the circumstances.

Ex. 7a
C. P. E. Bach, Türk   Marpurg

Ex. 7b
K. 13 Presto

[Witvogel: *t* instead of **m**]

K. 18** Presto

[Witvogel: trills *t*]

Ex. 8
K. 131 All°

[Venice: no ♮ before *d'* in bar 34; trills in 35 and 36 missing; middle-voice *f'* and *e♮'* in 39 absent]
[Parma: trills ⁓ , but the sign missing in 38

K. 491** Allegro

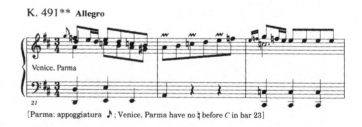

[Parma: appoggiatura ♪ ; Venice, Parma have no ♮ before *C* in bar 23]

K. 526* Allegro Comodo

[Venice: bass in bar 15 wrongly copied as *g*, but tie and *b♭* in 16 match Parma]

---

[8] C. P. E. Bach, *Versuch*, Chap. II, Sec. iii, §30; Marpurg, *Anleitung*, p. 57; Türk, *Klavierschule*, Chap. IV, §55-57. Although C. P. E. Bach's and Türk's examples show the main note starting a fraction of a second behind, what we hear is virtually the same as the main-note start on the beat.

[9] C. P. E. Bach (ibid., Sec. iv, §14 and 17) said that few people, aside from keyboard players, were familiar with the sign for the turn, and that the trill sign was used for it. Türk expresses a similar opinion (ibid., §75).

ACCIACCATURA AND ARPEGGIO

The *acciaccatura* (*acciaccare* means "to crush") is a decorating device effected by inserting a nonharmonic tone or tones into a consonant chord. It is played either in arpeggio or simultaneous fashion.

(a) A nonharmonic note inserted in broken-chord style:

Francesco Gasparini discusses this type of accessory note in conjunction with recitative accompaniment, and he makes a distinction between *mordente* (*mordere* means "to bite") and *acciaccatura*.[10] The former denotes an accessory note ascending a half step, for which Gasparini shows bass figures of $\sharp_{2}^{5}{}_{3}$, $\sharp_{5}^{78}$, $\sharp_{3}^{56}$ (**Ex. 9a**). *Acciaccatura*, though his explanation is less clear, seems to apply to all accessory notes other than the *mordente* (**Ex. 9b**). Both *mordente* and *acciaccatura* are to be played on or slightly ahead of the beat and are shown in black to indicate shorter duration than white notes. Geminiani's distinction between *tatto* (or *tacto*, which, according to him, means to touch the key lightly and release it immediately as if it were on fire) and *acciaccatura* (both are notated in black) corresponds to Gasparini's distinction between *mordente* and *acciaccatura*.[11]

Numerous French composers show similar passing dissonances with different signs under diverse names (**Ex. 9c**). J. S. Bach uses such an accessory note in his keyboard works (**Ex. 9d**), which is explained by C. P. E. Bach, Marpurg, Türk, among others (**Ex. 9e**). [12]

Ex. 9a

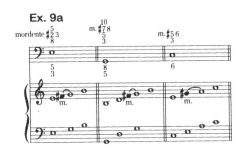

Ex. 9b

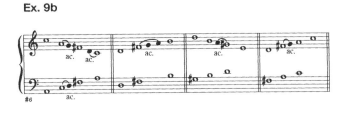

Ex. 9c

D'Anglebert   Rameau   G. Le Roux   F. Couperin

Cheute sur une notte | Cheute sur 2 nottes | Arpègement figuré | Coulé sur une tierce | Autre | Tierce coulée, en montant | Tierce coulée, en descendant

Ex. 9d
J. S. Bach
Partita No. 6, Sarabande   English Suite No. 1, Sarabande

Ex. 9e
C. P. E. Bach   Marpurg   Türk

---

[10] *L'armonico pratico al cimbalo* (Venice, 1708), Chap. IX. Gasparini says that the *mordente* is like the bite of a small animal that releases its hold as soon as it bites so as not to cause harm, and that it is suitable before the notes of a minor third, an octave, and a major sixth. It is quoted in Frank T. Arnold's *The Art of Accompaniment from a Thorough Bass* (New York, 1965), Vol. I, Chap II §4.

[11] *A Treatise of Good Taste*, Introduction (London, 1749).

[12] *Versuch*, I, Chap. III, §26; *Anleitung*, p. 60 (*Principes*, p. 70) and Tab. V, 18 & 20; *Klavierschule*, Chap. IV, §68, respectively. A passing *acciaccatura* bridging two consonant notes a third apart is similar to the slide (*Schleifer* or *coulé*).

Scarlatti's passing *acciaccatura* is indicated by either a small or a regular note (**Ex. 10**).

(b) Simultaneously struck nonharmonic note(s) in a chord:

Gasparini explains this as a harmonic clash in the progression $^{6}_{4}$$^{5}_{3}$. The left-hand parts, although doubling those of the right hand, maintain the fourth instead of resolving to the major third, while the right-hand part resolves. According to him, it is a kind of *acciaccatura*, and it creates a pleasing harmony on the harpsichord (**Ex. 11**).[13]

C. P. E. Bach and Marpurg (**Ex. 12a**)[14] and Türk (**Ex. 12b**)[15] also give similar examples, but they show the lower dissonant note being released sooner than the main note; and both C. P. E. Bach and Marpurg call this usage a special manner of executing a very short mordent.

In Scarlatti's works, especially those with early Kirkpatrick numbers, the so-called simultaneous *acciaccature* are plentiful, and they generate harmonic and dynamic intensity. As in his father A. Scarlatti's practice,

Ex. 10

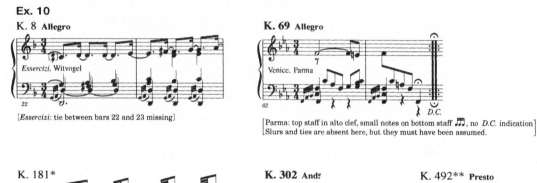

[*Essercizi*: tie between bars 22 and 23 missing]

[Parma: top staff in alto clef, small notes on bottom staff ♫, no *D.C.* indication]
[Slurs and ties are absent here, but they must have been assumed.]

[Parma: All^o]

Ex. 11   A. Scarlatti   A. Scarlatti

Ex. 12a   **Ex. 12b**
C. P. E. Bach   Türk
Marpurg

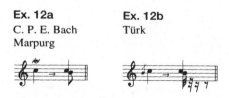

---

[13] *L'armonico*, Chap. VI, quoted by Arnold (p. 254) along with A. Scarlatti's examples.
[14] *Versuch*, I, Chap. II, Sec. v. §3; *Anleitung*, p. 58*f* (*Principes*, p. 64*f*).
[15] *Klavierschule*, Chap. IV, §66.

the left-hand part stays on the fourth (**Ex. 13a**). But this technique is also applied to other intervals as well (**Ex. 13b**). The dissonance may appear with no preparation (**Ex. 13c**) or with no resolution (K. 115** in Ex. 13b) or as simultaneous striking of what Le Roux and Couperin termed *coulé* and *tierce coulée* respectively (**Ex. 13d**). When multiple dissonances are inserted into a series of dense chords, the resulting sound is astoundingly loud, bold, and complex (**Ex. 13e**).

As for the arpeggio, some composers used specific signs, like ⦃ or ⦄ or ⌐⌐ for downward and upward arpeggiation of a chord respectively, while others indicated more generally ⦙ or such words as *arpeggio* or *Harpegg*.

Yet others simply assumed that performers ought to understand the proper context for the arpeggio, even without any markings.

Arpeggio signs are totally absent in Scarlatti's music, except for a few written-out examples (see Scarlatti's Ornaments and Their Performance, Part I, in Volume II, Ex. 1, K. 394**). The paucity of directives from the composer, however, does not mean that the notes of chords are always to be struck together. This is also true of his simultaneous *acciaccature*. By rolling the chords very briskly (in Ex. 13a, **K. 64**; Ex. 13c, K. 141*) rather than simply pounding them together, the passionate character of the pieces will be greatly enhanced.

Ex. 13a
K. 24* Presto

K. 64 All.º

Ex. 13b
K. 68

[Worgan: **Allegro**]

K. 115 All.º

[Parma: tenor *c'* in bar 2 dotted quarter-note]

Ex. 13c
K. 141* Allegro

[Münster: no tempo indication, but titled as 'Toccata';
tenor in bars 1 and 2 *f*s, not *g*s

Ex. 13d
K. 181*

[Parma: All.º]

Ex. 13e
K. 119** Allegro

See also K. 175** in Volume II, Scarlatti's Ornaments and Their Performance, Part I, Ex. 15.

EMBELLISHING A PHRASE IN ITS REPEAT

For a phrase or a piece to be elaborately embellished like a variation at its repeat was a common practice in the baroque period. A. Corelli, J. S. Bach, Quantz, and C. P. E. Bach, among others, applied this technique to their own works and/or explained how to bring a successful result from this method. F. Tosi even claimed that a singer who does not vary an aria in its repeat is not a great master.[16]

Scarlatti also introduced this technique in some of his sonatas (**Ex. 14**). The examples shown here are not of highly elaborate decorations, but the original melody is intact and is embroidered with a few extra notes. It is possible that he occasionally used such a technique in an improvisatory manner as he performed his own sonatas.

2001 (Revised 2011)

Ex. 14

[Parma: *Tremulo* above bars 29, 31]

[Ties in Venice and Parma are exactly as shown here]

---

[16] *Opinioni*, Chap. VII, §4.

ACKNOWLEDGEMENTS

I am indebted to the Rockefeller Foundation for inviting me to spend a month as a Resident at their Center in Bellagio, Italy, during the spring of 1998 while I was working on these ninety sonatas by Domenico Scarlatti. The three-volume set was published by Zen-On Music Co. of Tokyo between 1999 and 2002, but Dover Publications' interest and efforts in publishing this newly revised version of the edition are particularly appreciated. My gratitude also extends to Dr. Joel Sheveloff of Boston University and to my former colleagues at the University of Cincinnati, but especially to my wife, Ruth, for her invaluable assistance.

I only regret that my former teacher and mentor, Professor Ralph Kirkpatrick of Yale University, who encouraged me to publish more of Scarlatti's sonatas and turned over to me his own Scarlatti materials, did not live to see this edition.

2012

Sonata in G Major, K. 337

Sources: Venice VII 12, Parma IX 10, Münster IV 59, Vienna One B 57

22

Sonata in G Major, K. 338

Sources: Venice VII 13, Parma IX 11, Münster III 1, Vienna One E 1

25

26

Sonata in A Major, K. 343

Sources: Venice VII 18, Parma IX 16, Münster IV 63

Sonata in A Major, K. 344

Sources: Venice VII 19, Parma IX 17, Münster IV 64

Sonata in D Major, K. 358

Sources: Venice VIII 1, Parma X 11

Sonata in D Major, K. 359

Sources: Venice VIII 2, Parma X 12

42

Sonata in B-flat Major, K. 360

Sources: Venice VIII 3, Parma IX 25, Münster II 9

46

47

Sonata in B-flat Major, K. 361

Sources: Venice VIII 4, Parma IX 26, Münster II 10

Allegrissimo

LXVIII

49

50

Sonata in E-flat Major, K. 370

Sources: Venice VIII 13, Parma X 13, Münster III 35, Vienna One E 31

54

55

Sonata in E-flat Major, K. 371

Sources: Venice VIII 14, Parma X 14, Münster III 36, Vienna One E 32

Allegro

LXX

[L]

58

Sonata in A Minor, K. 382

Sources: Venice VIII 25, Parma X 25

Sonata in A Minor, K. 383

Sources: Venice VIII 26, Parma X 26

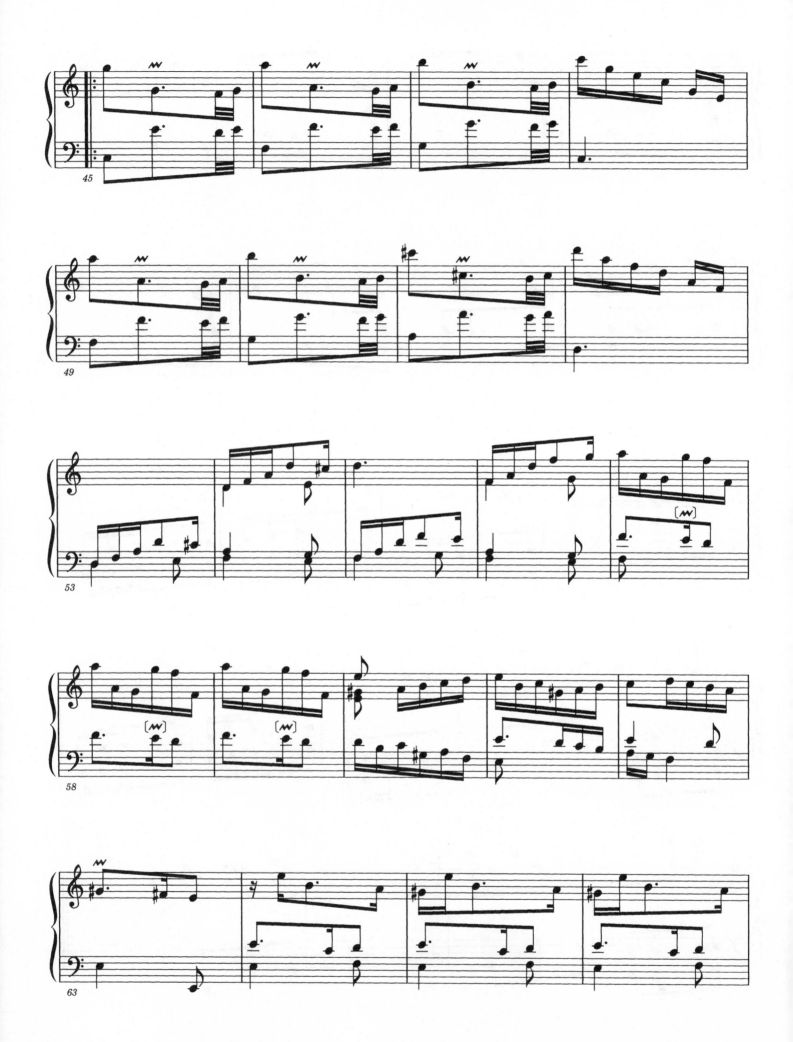

66

Sonata in F Minor, K. 386

Sources: Venice VIII 29, Parma X 29, Münster IV 67, Cambridge 12 15

Sonata in F Minor, K. 387

Sources: Venice VIII 30, Parma X 30, Münster IV 68, Cambridge 12 18

Veloce e fugato

Sonata in G Major, K. 412

Sources: Venice IX 25, Parma XI 25, Münster III 53, Vienna One F 1

Sonata in G Major, K. 413

Sources: Venice IX 26, Parma XI 26, Münster III 54, Vienna One F 2

Sonata in F Major, K. 418

Sources: Venice X 1, Parma XI 27, Münster III 55, Vienna One F 3

84

Sonata in F Major, K. 419

Sources: Venice X 2, Parma XI 28, Münster III 56, Vienna One F 4

Sonata in F Minor, K. 481

Sources: Venice XI 28, Parma XIII 27, Münster I 15, Vienna One G 32, Vienna Two Q. 15114 3, Vienna Two Q. 11432 I 3

92

Sonata in F Major, K. 482

Sources: Venice XI 29, Parma XIII 28, Münster I 16, Vienna One G 31, Vienna Two Q. 15114 4, Vienna Two Q. 11432 I 4

94

97

Sonata in F Major, K. 483

Sources: Venice XI 30, Parma XIII 29, Münster I 17, Vienna One G 29,
Vienna Two Q. 15114 5, Vienna Two Q. 11432 I 5

98

Sonata in D Major, K. 484

Sources: Venice XII 1, Parma XIV 1, Münster I 19, Vienna One C 15

Sonata in B-flat Major, K. 503

Sources: Venice XII 20, Parma XIV 20, Münster I 40, Vienna One C 35

108

Sonata in B-flat Major, K. 504

Sources: Venice XII 21, Parma XIV 21, Münster I 41, Vienna One C 36

Allegro

LXXXIV

Sonata in D Major, K. 509

Sources: Venice XII 26, Parma XIV 26, Münster I 32, Vienna One C 27

116

Sonata in D Minor, K. 510

Sources: Venice XII 27, Parma XIV 27, Münster I 33, Vienna One C 28

120

Sonata in E Major, K. 530

Sources: Venice XIII 17, Parma XV 17, Münster I 65, Vienna One D 15

124

Sonata in E Major, K. 531

Sources: Venice XIII 18, Parma XV 18, Münster I 66, Vienna One D 16

Allegro

LXXXVIII

128

Sonata in F Major, K. 540

Sources: Venice XIII 27, Parma XV 27, Münster I 75, Vienna One D 25

132

Sonata in F Major, K. 541

Sources: Venice XIII 28, Parma XV 28, Münster I 76, Vienna One D 26

DOMENICO SCARLATTI, NINETY SONATAS Volume III
Catalogue and Source Numbers

Ninety Sonatas	Key	Kirk-patrick	Longo	Manuscripts					
				Venice	Parma	Münster	Vienna I	Vienna II	Cambridge
LXI	G	337	Suppl.26	VII (1754) 12	IX (1754) 10	IV 59	B 57		
LXII	G	338	87	13	11	III 1	E 1		
LXIII	A	343	291	18	16	IV 63			
LXIV	A	344	295	19	17	64			
LXV	D	358	412	VIII (1754) 1	X (1754) 11				
LXVI	D	359	448	2	12				
LXVII	B♭	360	400	3	IX 25	II 9			
LXVIII	B♭	361	247	4	26	10			
LXIX	E♭	370	316	13	X 13	III 35	E 31		
LXX	E♭	371	17	14	14	36	32		
LXXI	a	382	Suppl.33	25	25				
LXXII	a	383	134	26	26				
LXXIII	f	386	171	29	29	IV 67			12 15
LXXIV	f	387	175	30	30	68			18
LXXV	G	412	182	IX (1754) 25	XI (1754) 25	III 53	F 1		
LXXVI	G	413	125	26	26	54	2		
LXXVII	F	418	26	X (1755) 1	27	55	3		
LXXVIII	F	419	279	2	28	56	4		
LXXIX	f	481	187	XI (1756) 28	XIII (1756) 27	I 15	G 32	Q. 15114 3 / Q. 11432 I 3	
LXXX	F	482	435	29	28	16	31	Q. 15114 4 / Q. 11432 I 4	
LXXXI	F	483	472	30	29	17	29	Q. 15114 5 / Q. 11432 I 5	
LXXXII	D	484	419	XII (1756) 1	XIV (1756) 1	19	C 15		
LXXIII	B♭	503	196	20	20	40	35		
LXXXIV	B♭	504	29	21	21	41	36		
LXXXV	D	509	311	26	26	32	27		
LXXXVI	d	510	277	27	27	33	28		
LXXXVII	E	530	44	XIII (1757) 17	XV (1757) 17	65	D 15		
LXXXVIII	E	531	430	18	18	66	16		
LXXXIX	F	540	Suppl.17	27	27	75	25		
XC	F	541	120	28	28	76	26		

NOTES ON THE TEXT OF THE SONATAS
Volume III

The location of discrepant notes, accidentals, etc. among the sources is presented here in the following order (not every item is present in all annotations): bar number / whether top or bottom staff / whether note(s) is (are) upstemmed or downstemmed / location of the note(s) within the bar (including appoggiaturas in small notation) / source(s) concerned.

The sources are identified by their respective names (Venice, Parma, Münster, Vienna I, etc.).

In the present edition, first and second endings are labelled *a* and *b* respectively (e.g., Sonata LXVII K. 360, bars 54a and 54b). Such separate endings are not clearly marked in the sources; instead, bowed lines appear over and under the notes. But the meaning of these bowed lines at the page turn can be ambiguous and puzzling. In such sonatas as LXI K. 337, LXXVII K. 418, and LXXXII K. 484, the idea of two separate endings is inappropriate, as skipping the first of the two bars and jumping to the second half of the sonata will not properly resolve the dominant chord to its tonic chord. While I cite each of these instances individually, these bowed lines may be merely a reminder that the piece still continues.

As mentioned earlier in Sources under B, sonatas in Parma XIV and XV often show the initial *S.* to the immediate right of the concluding bar (see facsimile page from K. 504 at front of this volume).

Pitches are identified by the following system:

Sonata LXI, K. 337

Bar 17 / bottom staff / Parma, Münster, Vienna I: no fermata.

Bar 25 / bottom / 1 / Münster, Vienna I: both *c'* and *c* dotted half-notes.

Bars 30, 32, 71 / bottom / 1 / Münster, Vienna I: ⲣ˙ with no rest (though in 69, it is difficult to determine whether it is a half rest or a dot next to the half note).

Bar 38 / top / 1 / Venice: soprano *f♯"* has no dot.

Bar 44 / Venice, Parma: | 8 :‖: but bar 45 | 8 :‖: has nothing;

Münster, Vienna I: no bowed lines.

Bar 66 / bottom / 1 / Münster, Vienna I: all three voices dotted.

Bar 83 / top / 1 / Parma: dot between *b'* and *g'* ; Münster, Vienna I: both *b'* and *g'* dotted.

Sonata LXII, K. 338

Bar 19 / bottom / 1 / Parma: *d'* has no dot.

Bar 37 / top / downstem / 1 / Münster, Vienna I: both *c♯"* and *a'* are dotted quarter-notes (though in bar 46, Münster, like Venice and Parma, has no dots); Vienna I: two dots have been crossed out.

Bar 48 / bottom / 3: ♯ from Münster and Vienna I.

Bars 56, 57 / Venice, Parma:

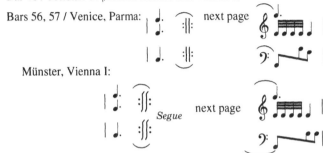

Münster, Vienna I:

Bar 80 / top / 1: ⁓ from Münster.

Bar 94 / top / downstem / 1 / Venice: *f♯"* has no dot. Münster, Vienna I: tenor *d"* absent.

Sonata LXIII, K. 343

Bar 18 / top: naturals in parentheses from Münster.

Bars 35, 36 /
Venice, Parma, Münster: | o :‖: next page

Bar 48 / top / upstem / 4 / Münster: *f♯"* quarter note.

Sonata LXIV, K. 344

- Added accidental: bar 32 / top / 5: ♮ before appoggiatura *d".*

Bar 12 / top / 1 / Parma, Münster: no ⁓ .

Bar 29 / top / 2: Münster has precautionary ♯ .

Bar / 53 / top / 1 / Münster: sixteenth-appoggiatura *d♯'* precedes final note.

Bar 68 / top / 1-3 / Venice: ▬▬ ; Parma, Münster: ▬▬ (Münster has no numeral 3).

Sonata LXV, K. 358

Bar 7 / bottom / 1 / Venice, Parma: position of dot between *c♯'* and *a* makes it difficult to determine to which note it applies. The present reading is based on bar 36.

Bars 59-62 / Venice: two-bar phrase appears one more time to make it three times.

Sonata LXVI, K. 359

Bar 102 / top and bottom / Parma: ⌒ over the rests.

Sonata LXVII, K. 360

- Münster: *Allegretto*.

Bar 29 / bottom / Parma: fermata above half-note *C*.

Bars 54a and b / Venice: [musical notation] next page [musical notation]

Parma: similar to Venice, but ⌒ above whole notes in 54a;

Münster: [musical notation] *Segue* next page [musical notation]

[1.] [2.] and dotted line with two dots for repeat sign between 54b and 55 are editorial additions.

Bar 55 / bottom / upstem / 2 / Münster: ♭ before *e'* (and ♮ before *e'* in bar 58).

Bar 67 / top / Parma, Münster: ⌣ above eighth-note *bb'*.

Bars 85-86 / top: tie from Münster.

Bars 105, 106 / top / downstem / 1 / Münster: *d'* is dotted half-note.

Bar 107 / Venice, Parma: [musical notation] *no* Münster: [musical notation] *Fine*

Adjustments have been made for smoother repetition of the half.

Sonata LXVIII, K. 361

- Slurs over or under thirty-second notes are inconsistent. Omission of slurs in Venice: bars 43, 45, 65, 86; in Parma: bars 43, 64, 65; in Münster: bars 56, 57, 61, 64, 65.

- Beams in Parma, Münster: [musical notation] in bars 45, 65, 84, 86 (Venice, has similar beaming only in 86).

Bar 4 / top / 4 / Münster: ⌣ instead of appoggiatura.

Bar 9 / bottom / 3 / Münster: ♭ before *d'*.

Bar 29 / bottom / 1 / Parma, Münster: *C* absent.

Bar 68 / top / beat 3: no note or rest here in any source.

Sonata LXIX, K. 370

Bar 9 / top / 4 / Münster, Vienna I: *c"*, not *d"*.

Bar 35 / Parma: fermata above *bb'*; Münster, Vienna I: ⌒ above *bb'* and below *Bb*.

Bars 37-39, 43-46 / top / upstem / all sources: [musical notation], which has been changed to [musical notation] (likewise, bar 17 / top / upstem / 2 / all sources: [musical notation], revised to [musical notation]).

Bar 78 / Parma: ⌒ above notes on each staff.

Sonata LXX, K. 371

Bars 14, 17 / all sources: *f♯* and *f♯*'s have additional ♯ to make two sharps, which I changed to *f×* and *f×*'s (see Editorial Policy, 3(a)).

Bar 28 / top / downstem / 3: precautionary ♮ from Parma, Münster, Vienna I.

Bar 59 / top / Parma: ⌒; Münster: fermata above each note.

Bar 61 / top / downstem / 3 / Venice: *c"*, not *d"*; Münster: *c"*s in both 61 and 63; Vienna I: *c"*s in 61 and 63 have been crossed out and replaced with *d"*s (with question mark over 61).

Bar 93 / top / 4 / Venice: no ⌣.

Sonata LXXI, K. 382

- Added accidentals: bar 7 / top / 1: ♯ before *g'*; bar 45 / top / upstem / last note: *d♮"*.

Bar 25 / top / Venice, Parma: ⌣ over *c"*, which has been moved to *d"*.

Bar 42 / top / 1: appoggiatura only in Parma.

Sonata LXXII, K. 383

Bars 49-51 / top / 2 / Parma: no ⌣.

Sonata LXXIII, K. 386

- Cambridge: no hand indications.

Bar 4 / 1 / all sources: *f'* appears as [musical notation].

Bars 34, 38, 77 / top / 1: appoggiatura from Cambridge.

Bar 35 / top / 5-7 / Münster, Cambridge: [musical notation] (bar 78 / Münster: likewise).

Bar 36 / top / 1 / Cambridge: eighth-appoggiatura *c"* present.

Bars 44, 45 /

Venice, Parma: [musical notation] next page [musical notation]

Münster: like Venice and Parma, but *C* in 45 is half note. Cambridge: eighth-appoggiatura *b(♮)'* before *c"*. ⌒ above *c"* as well as *C* in 44, but no bowed lines in either bar, and bass *C* absent in 45.

Bar 63 / top / 2 / Venice: unlike 69, *D* (for right) missing.

Bar 78 / top / 1 / Cambridge: [musical notation]

Bar 87 / Cambridge: ⌒ over whole note on each staff.

Sonata LXXIV, K. 387

- Venice: *Veloce è fugato*; Parma: *Veloce e fugato*; Münster: *Veloce*; Cambridge: *Veloce è fuga*.

Bars 2, 4 / bottom / 1 / Venice, Parma: *G₁*, not *F₁* (maybe the range of the instrument was limited, which necessitated short-octave tuning for this piece to produce *F₁* by tuning

G_1 to the pitch F_1; Münster, Cambridge: F_1.

Bar 5 / top / 1 / Parma, Münster: trill present.

Bars 18-19 / bottom / 2-1 / Cambridge: $A\flat$ and G, not $a\flat$ and g.

Bars 23, 27, 31, 55 / top / downstem / 2-3 / Venice, Parma: tie for downstem notes missing (Venice: tie for downstem notes in bar 35 also missing); (⌣) in 23 from Cambridge and in 27, 31, 55 from Münster and Cambridge.

Bars 28-30, 32-34, 60-62, 64-66 / top / beats 4-6 / all sources: ♩♩♩, which I changed to ♩♩♩ in order to avoid cumbersome appearance of long stem (bar 63 / top / 1-3 / all sources: likewise).

Bar 40 / top / 1 / Venice: no trill.

Bar 63 / top / 3-4: only Cambridge has ties.

Sonata LXXV, K. 412

- Added accidentals: bar 18 / bottom / 1: ♯ before c' (Vienna I has it); bars 66, 67 / bottom / upstem: $c\sharp'$ (Parma has ♯ in 66; Münster and Vienna I have ♯ before c's from 64 through 67, and ♮ before c' and c in 69).

- Vienna I: no tempo marking.

Bar 7 / top / downstem / 1 / Parma, Münster, Vienna I: alto g' absent.

Bar 23 / bottom / 3: precautionary ♮ from Münster, Vienna I.

Bars 29, 31, 50, 83, 85 / top / downstem / 1 / Münster, Vienna I: no trill.

Bar 34 / top / 4-5 / Venice: ↷ could be a tied trill, or ⌒ and ∿ written one on top of the other over $c\sharp''$.

Bar 50 / top / downstem / 1: Venice is only source to have trill.

Bar 51 / all sources: (musical example) (but no bowed lines in bar 52).

Bar 77 / top / 1: ∿ from Münster and Vienna I.

Bar 77 / bottom / last chord / all sources: unlike bar 75, bass D absent—only two voices, d and B appear.

Bars 80-81 / bottom / Venice: no tie.

Bar 87 / top / downstem / Venice: dotted quarter-note; Parma: dot in 91; Münster, Vienna I: dot in 37, 87, 91.

Bar 94 / top / downstem / 1 / Münster, Vienna I: $e\flat'$, not $f\sharp'$ (but upstem $e\flat''$ and $f\sharp''$ are as shown).

Bar 99 / top / downstem / 2 / Venice: ♭ missing.

Bar 105 / top / downstem / 1 / Münster, Vienna I: b', not g'.

Sonata LXXVI, K. 413

Bars 7-8 / bottom / upstem: tie in parentheses from Münster and Vienna I.

Bar 27 / Parma, Münster, Vienna I: (musical example) (but no bowed lines in 28); Venice: no bowed lines in either bar.

Sonata LXXVII, K. 418

- Added accidental: bar 38 / top / 1: ♮ before bb' (Parma has it).

- Venice, Parma: dots for staccato appear inconsistently. In the first half, they are completely absent altogether in the left-hand part, as is dot for the initial note of ascending lines in the right. In the second half, corresponding passages fare a little better. Münster, Vienna I: absence of dots is more extensive in the second half.

Bar 10 / bottom / 4: ♮ before bb' is erased in Münster, omitted in Vienna I.

Bars 52, 53 /
Venice, Parma, Münster: (musical example)   next page (musical example)

Vienna I: no bowed lines.

Bar 55 / top / last note: ♭ from Münster and Vienna I.

Bars 61-62 / bottom / Venice: no dots for the quarter notes (dots also missing in bar 86 / top / last note, and in 87, 89, 95 / bottom / 2, 3).

Bars 64, 65 / Münster, Vienna I: ♮ before b and b' in respective bars.

Bar 93 / bottom / last note: dot from Münster and Vienna I.

Bar 96 / top / Parma: dots missing.

Bar 98 / all sources: dots absent.

Sonata LXXVIII, K. 419

- *Più tosto presto che Allegro* (closer to *Presto* than *Allegro*).

Bar 24 / top / 2 / Venice: no ∿ .

Bars 34-35 / top: tie between c''s from Münster and Vienna I.

Bar 57 / top / upstem / Venice, Parma: (musical example). I followed Münster, Vienna I version, which has the same rhythmic pattern as bar 52.

Bar 103 / bottom / upstem / 1, 2 / Münster, Vienna I: no tenor part (like bar 113).

Bars 103-104, 113-114 / bottom / Münster: tie between fs; Vienna I: tie between fs only 113-114.

Bar 108 / top / downstem / 2 / Vienna I: ♭ before a', not ♮; Münster: ♮ was changed to ♭ by solution.

Sonata LXXIX, K. 481

- Added accidental: bar 41 / bottom / upstem / 1: ♮ before $a\flat'$ (last note has ♮ in all sources).

- Venice: *And.ᵉ è Cantabbile*; Parma: *And.ᵉ e Cantabbile*; Münster, Vienna I G32, Vienna II Q. 11432: *Andante Cantabile*; Q. 15114: unclear.

Bar 3 / bottom / beat 1: Münster, Vienna I, Q. 15114, Q. 11432: quarter-note f' present, just like bar 1.

Bar 4 / top / 2: ∿ from Münster.

Bars 6, 13, 15, 16 / top / all sources: [♪♩ ♩ ♫], changed to [♪♩ ♪♫♫].

Bars 10, 12 / top / Venice, Parma, Münster, Q. 15114, Q. 11432: [♪ ♩.] 𝄽 ; Vienna I: [♩ ♩] and [♩ ♩.] 𝄽 respectively. I revised them all to [♫♩] 𝄽 .

Bar 13 / top / 6 / Venice: trill absent.

Bar 13 / top / 7: precautionary ♮ from Münster.

Bar 17 / top / 1 / Venice: appoggiatura missing.

Bar 19 / top / Münster: trill over quarter-note *f♯'*.

Bars 27, 28, 30, 31 / top / beat 2 / Münster: [♪♩♫], not [♪♫♫] ([♫] in bar 31).

Bars 31, 32 / top / Venice, Parma: triplets have already appeared often before, but numeral 3 (aside from that in bar 9) is seen only here.

Bar 31 / bottom / downstem / 3 / Münster: *f*, not *g* (like bar 28).

Bar 33 / top / 2: only Parma has *tr*.

Bar 34 / top / last note: trill only in Venice and Vienna I.

Bar 46 / bottom / downstem / 1: ♮ from Münster.

Bar 64 / top / last note / Venice: no ∿ .

Sonata LXXX, K. 482

-Vienna I: 𝄵, not ¢ .

Bar 4 / top / upstem / all sources [♩ ♩. ♫♫], changed to [♩ ♩♪♫♫] .

Bar 6 / top / upstem / Venice, Parma, Münster: [♩ ♩. ♫] ; Vienna I and II: [♩ ♩♪♫♫] .

Bar 38 / top / downstem / 2: ♭ from Münster.

Bars 41, 46, 83, 88 / top / upstem / 1 / all sources: while these hand designations look curious, they are what the sources show (Vienna I stops indicating *D* and *M* from 83 on).

Bar 46 / bottom / 1: *M* only in Q. 15114 and Q. 11432.

Bars 52, 53 /

Venice, Parma, Münster: [music: repeat measures] next page [music: treble/bass clefs]

Vienna I and II: no bowed lines.

Bar 57 / Venice: this bar appears twice.

Sonata LXXXI, K. 483

- Trill signs appear inconsistently. Those missing in Venice are: top / bars 57, 68, 91 and bottom / 30, 35, 37, 42, 43, 53, 54, 87, 97, 99; in Parma: top / bars 57, 68, 91 and bottom / 35, 42, 53, 87, 97, 99. In the secondary sources, absence of the sign is equally noticeable, but in Münster / top / 57, 68, 91 and bottom 35, 53, 87, 97, 99 (where Venice and Parma have no trill), *t* is present; in Vienna I / top / 68, 91 and bottom / 42, 53, 87, ∿ appears. In Q. 15114 and Q. 11432, locations of *t* basically correspond to those in Vienna I.

Bars 1, 4 / top / Venice, Parma: [music figure] ; Münster, Vienna I and II version [music figure] has been followed here.

Bar 17 / top / 2 : Münster is only source to have *c"* ; all others have *d"*. After comparing with adjacent bars and bar 73, as well as for harmonic reasons, I have taken the Münster version.

Bars 22, 24 / bottom / 5: all sources have ♯ only before the third note, but no renewed ♯ here. While interpreting it as *f♮* may be a possibility, bars 61 / top / 3, 62 / bottom / 3, 65 / bottom / 6, etc. show no renewed ♯ either. Hence, *f♯* must have been assumed here (as is *B♮* in bars 78, 80).

Bar 28 / top / Venice: no trill (Vienna I: trills for both hands).

Bar 68 / bottom / 5: ♮ from Münster.

Sonata LXXXII, K. 484

Bars 21-22 / top: tie between *c♯'''*'s from Münster and Vienna I.

Bars 65, 66 / all sources: [music: repeat measures] next page [music: treble/bass clefs]

Bar 78 / bottom / 1 / Venice: quarter-note *D* absent.

Bar 103 / bottom / Venice: *F♯*, not *G*.

Sonata LXXXIII, K. 503

Bar 25 / bottom / 3, 4 / Münster, Vienna I: tenor *e♭*'s throughout.

Bar 36 / downstem / 3: ♮ before *e'* from Münster and Vienna I.

Bar 37 / bottom / 1 / Parma: no ♯ before *C*.

Bars 43, 44 / all sources: [music: repeat measures] next page [music: treble/bass clefs]

Bar 50 / top / downstem / 1 / Münster, Vienna I: both *f♯'* on beat 4 and tie missing.

Sonata LXXXIV, K. 504

- Six sixteenth-notes in a bar are often divided into two groups in Venice and Parma (as in bars 12-26), possibly implying certain rhythmic emphasis. This is not the case in Münster and Vienna I, in which the six notes are almost always beamed together.

Bar 23 / top / Parma, Münster, Vienna I: no ∿ .

Bar 50 / top / Venice, Parma: [music figure] (unlike 49, 51); Münster, Vienna I version is taken here.

Bar 50 / top / upstem / 2: ♮ before *e♭"* from Münster and Vienna I.

Bar 54 / top / 1 / Venice: ∿ over *d"*.

Bar 72 / top / Venice: no ∿ .

Bar 79 / bottom / downstem / 1 / Venice, Parma: *f*; Münster, Vienna I: *eb*, which seems more logical.

Bar 87 / bottom / 1 / Parma, Münster, Vienna I: eighth-note *Eb* present.

Sonata LXXXV, K. 509

- Added accidentals: bars 33, 38 / top / last note: ♮ before *g''*.

Bars 14, 15 / top / upstem / all sources:  changed to ♪ ♩. which corresponds to bars 13 and 16.

Bar 20 / bottom / 2 / Venice: no ᷉.
Bar 27 / top / 4 / Venice: no trill.
Bars 47, 48 / Venice, Parma, Münster: [notation] next page [notation]

Vienna I: ⌣ present in 48 but not in 47.

Bar 58 / top / Venice: [notation]

Parma: [notation] which has been taken.

Münster, Vienna I: like Parma, but with slurs between appoggiatura *f♯''*s and quarter-note *e''*s.

Sonata LXXXVI, K. 510

- Parma, Münster, Vienna I: *Allegro molto.*

- Venice, Parma: two naturals at the beginning of the sonata signify cancellation of D major from the preceding sonata (see Domenico Scarlatti and His Keyboard Music at the beginning of this volume).

- *tre.* only in Venice and Parma; Münster: ᷉ or *tr*, but bar 104 looks like *tre.*; Vienna I: *tr* .

Bars 6-7 / top: tie between *d''*s from Münster, Vienna I.
Bars 14, 16 / bottom / downstem / Venice, Parma: ♪ ♪ : Münster: black notehead *d'* seems to have been enlarged to make ♪ and *c♯'* revised to ♪ , although both notes are heavily smudged; Vienna I: clearly ♪ ♪ . After examining succeeding bars, I have chosen the latter version.
Bar 21 / top / downstem: Parma alone has dot next to *c''*.
Bars 38, 40 / bottom / Münster, Vienna I: tenor *a* is tied from the preceding bar and restruck on beat 3.
Bar 44 / top / beat 3 / Münster, Vienna I: quarter-note *e''* in alto (like top two parts in 46).
Bar 45 / top / 1 / Venice: appoggiatura missing; Münster: position of appoggiaturas in 45, 47, 49 unclear, as they are far from main note without ledger lines; Vienna I: appoggiaturas are *g''*s.

Bars 46-49 / Münster, Vienna I: tenor *a'* is restruck on beat 3 and tied to next note.
Bar 48 / top / 2 / Parma: *tr*, not *tre.*
Bar 56 / bottom / upstem / Venice: no dot.

Sonata LXXXVII, K. 530

- Added accidental: bar 53 / top / 1: ♯ before *a'*.

Bar 26 / top / downstem / 1 / Münster, Vienna I: ♪' .
Bar 31 / top / Münster, Vienna I: dotted half-note *f♯'* present for the middle voice.
Bar 33 / top / 1 / Venice, Parma: appoggiatura *a'* : Münster: *f♯'*; Vienna I: curiously, *g'*.
Bar 52 / Münster, Vienna I: this bar absent, i.e., the one-bar phrase appears only three times, instead of four.
Bars 63-66 / Münster, Vienna I: all *g''*s and *g'* preceded by ♭.
Bar 80 / top / Venice, Parma: ᷉ over dotted eighth-note; Münster, Vienna I: ᷉ on beat 2.
Bar 82 / top / Venice: ᷉ missing.

Sonata LXXXVIII, K. 531

- Added accidental: bar 56 / top / 1: ♯ before *a*.

- Enharmonic changes: bars 59, 60, 61 / all sources: *f♯*'s and *f♯* (already sharped in key signature) have additional sharp to make two sharps, which have been changed to *f𝄪*'s and *f𝄪*. Similarly, bars 65, 66 / all sources: *c♯*'s with another ♯ have been revised to *c𝄪*'s (see Editorial Policy, 3(a)).

Sonata LXXXIX, K. 540

- Added accidentals: bars 22, 46 / top / 1: ♮ before *bb'*.

- Münster, Vienna I: appoggiatura before triplets only in bars 38, 39.
Bar 7 / top / upstem / last note / Venice, Parma: *c'''*; Münster, Vienna I: *d'''*, which has been chosen.
Bar 8 / bottom / 2, 3 / Venice, Parma: *bb* and *a* respectively; Münster, Vienna I: *a* and *g*, which correspond to the notes in the ensuing bars and will avert parallel fifths.
Bar 38 / top: numeral 3 from Münster and Vienna I.
Bar 88 / top / 5 / Venice: ᷉ absent.

Sonata XC, K. 541

- Added accidental: bar 27 / top / 1: ♮ before *bb'*.

- *tr* is absent in many places, such as in Venice: bars 21 (beat 1), 61 and 65 (*c♯''*), 71 and 73 (*b♮'*), 75 (in both voices), and 95; in Parma: bars 21 and 23 (none present), 31 and 33 (missing on beat 4), 65, 71, 85 and 95 (none present) and some seem to have been erased. In Münster and Vienna I, it is difficult to tell whether they are signs or ink stains.

Bar 21 / top / 1: **tr** in parentheses from Münster, Vienna I.

Bars 51, 52 / all sources: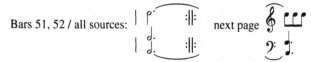

Bars 61, 63 / top / 1 / Venice, Parma :

Bar 90 / Venice: ⌢ above 𝄐 on each staff.

Dover Orchestral Scores

Bach, Johann Sebastian, COMPLETE CONCERTI FOR SOLO KEYBOARD AND ORCHESTRA IN FULL SCORE. Bach's seven complete concerti for solo keyboard and orchestra in full score from the authoritative Bach-Gesellschaft edition. 206pp. 9 x 12. 0-486-24929-8

Bach, Johann Sebastian, THE SIX BRANDENBURG CONCERTOS AND THE FOUR ORCHESTRAL SUITES IN FULL SCORE. Complete standard Bach-Gesellschaft editions in large, clear format. Study score. 273pp. 9 x 12. 0-486-23376-6

Bach, Johann Sebastian, THE THREE VIOLIN CONCERTI IN FULL SCORE. Concerto in A Minor, BWV 1041; Concerto in E Major, BWV 1042; and Concerto for Two Violins in D Minor, BWV 1043. Bach-Gesellschaft editions. 64pp. 9⅜ x 12¼. 0-486-25124-1

Beethoven, Ludwig van, COMPLETE PIANO CONCERTOS IN FULL SCORE. Complete scores of five great Beethoven piano concertos, with all cadenzas as he wrote them, reproduced from authoritative Breitkopf & Härtel edition. New Table of Contents. 384pp. 9⅜ x 12¼. 0-486-24563-2

Beethoven, Ludwig van, SIX GREAT OVERTURES IN FULL SCORE. Six staples of the orchestral repertoire from authoritative Breitkopf & Härtel edition. *Leonore Overtures,* Nos. 1–3; Overtures to *Coriolanus, Egmont, Fidelio.* 288pp. 9 x 12. 0-486-24789-9

Beethoven, Ludwig van, SYMPHONIES NOS. 1, 2, 3, AND 4 IN FULL SCORE. Republication of H. Litolff edition. 272pp. 9 x 12. 0-486-26033-X

Beethoven, Ludwig van, SYMPHONIES NOS. 5, 6 AND 7 IN FULL SCORE, Ludwig van Beethoven. Republication of H. Litolff edition. 272pp. 9 x 12. 0-486-26034-8

Beethoven, Ludwig van, SYMPHONIES NOS. 8 AND 9 IN FULL SCORE. Republication of H. Litolff edition. 256pp. 9 x 12. 0-486-26035-6

Beethoven, Ludwig van; Mendelssohn, Felix; and Tchaikovsky, Peter Ilyitch, GREAT ROMANTIC VIOLIN CONCERTI IN FULL SCORE. The Beethoven Op. 61, Mendelssohn Op. 64 and Tchaikovsky Op. 35 concertos reprinted from Breitkopf & Härtel editions. 224pp. 9 x 12. 0-486-24989-1

Borodin, Alexander, SYMPHONY NO. 2 IN B MINOR IN FULL SCORE. Rescored after its disastrous debut, the four movements offer a unified construction of dramatic contrasts in mood, color, and tempo. A beloved example of Russian nationalist music of the Romantic period. viii+152pp. 9 x 12. 0-486-44120-2

Brahms, Johannes, COMPLETE CONCERTI IN FULL SCORE. Piano Concertos Nos. 1 and 2; Violin Concerto, Op. 77; Concerto for Violin and Cello, Op. 102. Definitive Breitkopf & Härtel edition. 352pp. 9⅜ x 12¼. 0-486-24170-X

Brahms, Johannes, COMPLETE SYMPHONIES. Full orchestral scores in one volume. No. 1 in C Minor, Op. 68; No. 2 in D Major, Op. 73; No. 3 in F Major, Op. 90; and No. 4 in E Minor, Op. 98. Reproduced from definitive Vienna Gesellschaft der Musikfreunde edition. Study score. 344pp. 9 x 12. 0-486-23053-8

Brahms, Johannes, THREE ORCHESTRAL WORKS IN FULL SCORE: Academic Festival Overture, Tragic Overture and Variations on a Theme by Joseph Haydn. Reproduced from the authoritative Breitkopf & Härtel edition three of Brahms's great orchestral favorites. Editor's commentary in German and English. 112pp. 9⅜ x 12¼. 0-486-24637-X

Chopin, Frédéric, THE PIANO CONCERTOS IN FULL SCORE. The authoritative Breitkopf & Härtel full-score edition in one volume; Piano Concertos No. 1 in E Minor and No. 2 in F Minor. 176pp. 9 x 12. 0-486-25835-1

Corelli, Arcangelo, COMPLETE CONCERTI GROSSI IN FULL SCORE. All 12 concerti in the famous late nineteenth-century edition prepared by violinist Joseph Joachim and musicologist Friedrich Chrysander. 240pp. 8⅜ x 11¼. 0-486-25606-5

Debussy, Claude, THREE GREAT ORCHESTRAL WORKS IN FULL SCORE. Three of the Impressionist's most-recorded, most-performed favorites: *Prélude à l'Après-midi d'un Faune, Nocturnes,* and *La Mer.* Reprinted from early French editions. 279pp. 9 x 12. 0-486-24441-5

Dvořák, Antonín, SERENADE NO. 1, OP. 22, AND SERENADE NO. 2, OP. 44, IN FULL SCORE. Two works typified by elegance of form, intense harmony, rhythmic variety, and uninhibited emotionalism. 96pp. 9 x 12. 0-486-41895-2

Dvořák, Antonín, SYMPHONY NO. 8 IN G MAJOR, OP. 88, SYMPHONY NO. 9 IN E MINOR, OP. 95 ("NEW WORLD") IN FULL SCORE. Two celebrated symphonies by the great Czech composer, the Eighth and the immensely popular Ninth, "From the New World," in one volume. 272pp. 9 x 12. 0-486-24749-X

Elgar, Edward, CELLO CONCERTO IN E MINOR, OP. 85, IN FULL SCORE. A tour de force for any cellist, this frequently performed work is widely regarded as an elegy for a lost world. Melodic and evocative, it exhibits a remarkable scope, ranging from tragic passion to buoyant optimism. Reproduced from an authoritative source. 112pp. 8⅜ x 11. 0-486-41896-0

Franck, César, SYMPHONY IN D MINOR IN FULL SCORE. Superb, authoritative edition of Franck's only symphony, an often-performed and recorded masterwork of late French romantic style. 160pp. 9 x 12. 0-486-25373-2

Handel, George Frideric, COMPLETE CONCERTI GROSSI IN FULL SCORE. Monumental Opus 6 Concerti Grossi, Opus 3 and "Alexander's Feast" Concerti Grossi—19 in all—reproduced from the most authoritative edition. 258pp. 9⅜ x 12¼. 0-486-24187-4

Handel, George Frideric, WATER MUSIC AND MUSIC FOR THE ROYAL FIREWORKS IN FULL SCORE. Full scores of two of the most popular Baroque orchestral works performed today—reprinted from the definitive Deutsche Handelgesellschaft edition. Total of 96pp. 8⅛ x 11. 0-486-25070-9

Haydn, Joseph, SYMPHONIES 88–92 IN FULL SCORE: The Haydn Society Edition. Full score of symphonies Nos. 88 through 92. Large, readable noteheads, ample margins for fingerings, etc., and extensive Editor's Commentary. 304pp. 9 x 12. (Available in U.S. only) 0-486-24445-8

Mahler, Gustav, DAS LIED VON DER ERDE IN FULL SCORE. Mahler's masterpiece, a fusion of song and symphony, reprinted from the original 1912 Universal Edition. English translations of song texts. 160pp. 9 x 12. 0-486-25657-X

Mahler, Gustav, SYMPHONIES NOS. 1 AND 2 IN FULL SCORE. Unabridged, authoritative Austrian editions of Symphony No. 1 in D Major ("Titan") and Symphony No. 2 in C Minor ("Resurrection"). 384pp. 8⅛ x 11. 0-486-25473-9

Mahler, Gustav, SYMPHONIES NOS. 3 AND 4 IN FULL SCORE. Two brilliantly contrasting masterworks—one scored for a massive ensemble, the other for small orchestra and soloist—reprinted from authoritative Viennese editions. 368pp. 9⅜ x 12¼. 0-486-26166-2

Mahler, Gustav, SYMPHONY NO. 8 IN FULL SCORE. Authoritative edition of massive, complex "Symphony of a Thousand." Scored for orchestra, eight solo voices, double chorus, boys' choir and organ. Reprint of Izdatel'stvo "Muzyka," Moscow, edition. Translation of texts. 272pp. 9⅜ x 12¼. 0-486-26022-4

Mendelssohn, Felix, MAJOR ORCHESTRAL WORKS IN FULL SCORE. Considered to be Mendelssohn's finest orchestral works, here in one volume are the complete *Midsummer Night's Dream; Hebrides Overture; Calm Sea and Prosperous Voyage Overture;* Symphony No. 3 in A ("Scottish"); and Symphony No. 4 in A ("Italian"). Breitkopf & Härtel edition. Study score. 406pp. 9 x 12. 0-486-23184-4

*Available from your music dealer or write for **free** Music Catalog to*
Dover Publications, Inc., Dept. MUBI, 31 East 2nd Street, Mineola, NY 11501
*Visit us online at **www.doverpublications.com***

Dover Orchestral Scores

Mozart, Wolfgang Amadeus, CONCERTI FOR WIND INSTRUMENTS IN FULL SCORE. Exceptional volume contains ten pieces for orchestra and wind instruments and includes some of Mozart's finest, most popular music. 272pp. 9⅜ x 12¼. 0-486-25228-0

Mozart, Wolfgang Amadeus, LATER SYMPHONIES. Full orchestral scores to last symphonies (Nos. 35–41) reproduced from definitive Breitkopf & Härtel Complete Works edition. Study score. 285pp. 9 x 12.
0-486-23052-X

Mozart, Wolfgang Amadeus, PIANO CONCERTOS NOS. 1–6 IN FULL SCORE. Reproduced complete and unabridged from the authoritative Breitkopf & Hartel Complete Works edition, it offers a revealing look at the development of a budding master. x+198pp. 9⅜ x 12¼. 0-486-44191-1

Mozart, Wolfgang Amadeus, PIANO CONCERTOS NOS. 11–16 IN FULL SCORE. Authoritative Breitkopf & Härtel edition of six staples of the concerto repertoire, including Mozart's cadenzas for Nos. 12–16. 256pp. 9⅜ x 12¼.
0-486-25468-2

Mozart, Wolfgang Amadeus, PIANO CONCERTOS NOS. 17–22 IN FULL SCORE. Six complete piano concertos in full score, with Mozart's own cadenzas for Nos. 17–19. Breitkopf & Härtel edition. Study score. 370pp. 9⅜ x 12¼. 0-486-23599-8

Mozart, Wolfgang Amadeus, PIANO CONCERTOS NOS. 23–27 IN FULL SCORE. Mozart's last five piano concertos in full score, plus cadenzas for Nos. 23 and 27, and the Concert Rondo in D Major, K.382. Breitkopf & Härtel edition. Study score. 310pp. 9⅜ x 12¼. 0-486-23600-5

Mozart, Wolfgang Amadeus, 17 DIVERTIMENTI FOR VARIOUS INSTRUMENTS. Sparkling pieces of great vitality and brilliance from 1771 to 1779; consecutively numbered from 1 to 17. Reproduced from definitive Breitkopf & Härtel Complete Works edition. Study score. 241pp. 9⅜ x 12¼.
0-486-23862-8

Mozart, Wolfgang Amadeus, THE VIOLIN CONCERTI AND THE SINFONIA CONCERTANTE, K.364, IN FULL SCORE. All five violin concerti and famed double concerto reproduced from authoritative Breitkopf & Härtel Complete Works Edition. 208pp. 9⅜ x 12¼. 0-486-25169-1

Paganini, Nicolo and Wieniawski, Henri, PAGANINI'S VIOLIN CONCERTO NO. 1 IN D MAJOR, OP. 6, AND WIENIAWSKI'S VIOLIN CONCERTO NO. 2 IN D MINOR, OP. 22, IN FULL SCORE. This outstanding new edition brings together two of the most popular and most performed violin concertos of the Romantic repertoire in one convenient, moderately priced volume. 208pp. 8⅜ x 11. 0-486-43151-7

Ravel, Maurice, DAPHNIS AND CHLOE IN FULL SCORE. Definitive full-score edition of Ravel's rich musical setting of a Greek fable by Longus is reprinted here from the original French edition. 320pp. 9⅜ x 12¼. (Not available in France or Germany) 0-486-25826-2

Ravel, Maurice, LE TOMBEAU DE COUPERIN and VALSES NOBLES ET SENTIMENTALES IN FULL SCORE. *Le Tombeau de Couperin* consists of "Prelude," "Forlane," "Menuet," and "Rigaudon"; the uninterrupted 8 waltzes of *Valses Nobles et Sentimentales* abound with lilting rhythms and unexpected harmonic subtleties. 144pp. 9⅜ x 12¼. (Not available in France or Germany) 0-486-41898-7

Ravel, Maurice, RAPSODIE ESPAGNOLE, MOTHER GOOSE and PAVANE FOR A DEAD PRINCESS IN FULL SCORE. Full authoritative scores of 3 enormously popular works by the great French composer, each rich in orchestral settings. 160pp. 9⅜ x 12¼. 0-486-41899-5

Saint-Saens, Camille, DANSE MACABRE AND HAVANAISE FOR VIOLIN AND ORCHESTRA IN FULL SCORE. Two of Saint-Saens' most popular works appear in this affordable volume: the symphonic poem about the dance of death, *Danse Macabre,* and *Havanaise,* a piece inspired by a Cuban dance that highlights its languid mood with bursts of virtuosity. iv+92pp. 9 x 12. 0-486-44147-4

Schubert, Franz, FOUR SYMPHONIES IN FULL SCORE. Schubert's four most popular symphonies: No. 4 in C Minor ("Tragic"); No. 5 in B-flat Major; No. 8 in B Minor ("Unfinished"); and No. 9 in C Major ("Great"). Breitkopf & Härtel edition. Study score. 261pp. 9⅜ x 12¼. 0-486-23681-1

Schubert, Franz, SYMPHONY NO. 3 IN D MAJOR AND SYMPHONY NO. 6 IN C MAJOR IN FULL SCORE. The former is scored for 12 wind instruments and timpani; the latter is known as "The Little Symphony in C" to distinguish it from Symphony No. 9, "The Great Symphony in C." Authoritative editions. 128pp. 9⅜ x 12¼. 0-486-42134-1

Schumann, Robert, COMPLETE SYMPHONIES IN FULL SCORE. No. 1 in B-flat Major, Op. 38 ("Spring"); No. 2 in C Major, Op. 61; No. 3 in E-flat Major, Op. 97 ("Rhenish"); and No. 4 in D Minor, Op. 120. Breitkopf & Härtel editions. Study score. 416pp. 9⅜ x 12¼. 0-486-24013-4

Strauss, Johann, Jr., THE GREAT WALTZES IN FULL SCORE. Complete scores of eight melodic masterpieces: "The Beautiful Blue Danube," "Emperor Waltz," "Tales of the Vienna Woods," "Wiener Blut," and four more. Authoritative editions. 336pp. 8⅜ x 11¼. 0-486-26009-7

Strauss, Richard, TONE POEMS, SERIES I: DON JUAN, TOD UND VERKLARUNG, and DON QUIXOTE IN FULL SCORE. Three of the most often performed and recorded works in entire orchestral repertoire, reproduced in full score from original editions. 286pp. 9⅜ x 12¼. (Available in U.S. only) 0-486-23754-0

Strauss, Richard, TONE POEMS, SERIES II: TILL EULENSPIEGELS LUSTIGE STREICHE, "ALSO SPRACH ZARATHUSTRA," and EIN HELDENLEBEN IN FULL SCORE. Three important orchestral works, including very popular *Till Eulenspiegel's Merry Pranks,* reproduced in full score from original editions. Study score. 315pp. 9⅜ x 12¼. (Available in U.S. only) 0-486-23755-9

Stravinsky, Igor, THE FIREBIRD IN FULL SCORE (Original 1910 Version). Inexpensive edition of modern masterpiece, renowned for brilliant orchestration, glowing color. Authoritative Russian edition. 176pp. 9⅜ x 12¼. (Available in U.S. only) 0-486-25535-2

Stravinsky, Igor, PETRUSHKA IN FULL SCORE: Original Version. Full-score edition of Stravinsky's masterful score for the great Ballets Russes 1911 production of *Petrushka.* 160pp. 9⅜ x 12¼. (Available in U.S. only) 0-486-25680-4

Stravinsky, Igor, THE RITE OF SPRING IN FULL SCORE. Full-score edition of most famous musical work of the 20th century, created as a ballet score for Diaghilev's Ballets Russes. 176pp. 9⅜ x 12¼. (Available in U.S. only)
0-486-25857-2

Tchaikovsky, Peter Ilyitch, FOURTH, FIFTH AND SIXTH SYMPHONIES IN FULL SCORE. Complete orchestral scores of Symphony No. 4 in F Minor, Op. 36; Symphony No. 5 in E Minor, Op. 64; Symphony No. 6 in B Minor, "Pathetique," Op. 74. Study score. Breitkopf & Härtel editions. 480pp. 9⅜ x 12¼. 0-486-23861-X

Tchaikovsky, Peter Ilyitch, NUTCRACKER SUITE IN FULL SCORE. Among the most popular ballet pieces ever created; available in a complete, inexpensive, high-quality score to study and enjoy. 128pp. 9 x 12.
0-486-25379-1

von Weber, Carl Maria, GREAT OVERTURES IN FULL SCORE. Overtures to *Oberon, Der Freischutz, Euryanthe* and *Preciosa* reprinted from authoritative Breitkopf & Härtel editions. 112pp. 9 x 12. 0-486-25225-6

*Available from your music dealer or write for **free** Music Catalog to*
Dover Publications, Inc., Dept. MUBI, 31 East 2nd Street, Mineola, NY 11501
*Visit us online at **www.doverpublications.com***

Dover Piano and Keyboard Editions

Albeniz, Isaac, IBERIA AND ESPAÑA: Two Complete Works for Solo Piano. Spanish composer's greatest piano works in authoritative editions. Includes the popular "Tango." 192pp. 9 x 12. 0-486-25367-8

Bach, Johann Sebastian, COMPLETE KEYBOARD TRANSCRIPTIONS OF CONCERTOS BY BAROQUE COMPOSERS. Sixteen concertos by Vivaldi, Telemann and others, transcribed for solo keyboard instruments. Bach-Gesellschaft edition. 128pp. 9⅜ x 12¼. 0-486-25529-8

Bach, Johann Sebastian, COMPLETE PRELUDES AND FUGUES FOR ORGAN. All 25 of Bach's complete sets of preludes and fugues (i.e. compositions written as pairs), from the authoritative Bach-Gesellschaft edition. 168pp. 8⅜ x 11. 0-486-24816-X

Bach, Johann Sebastian, ITALIAN CONCERTO, CHROMATIC FANTASIA AND FUGUE AND OTHER WORKS FOR KEYBOARD. Sixteen of Bach's best-known, most-performed and most-recorded works for the keyboard, reproduced from the authoritative Bach-Gesellschaft edition. 112pp. 9 x 12. 0-486-25387-2

Bach, Johann Sebastian, KEYBOARD MUSIC. Bach-Gesellschaft edition. For harpsichord, piano, other keyboard instruments. English Suites, French Suites, Six Partitas, Goldberg Variations, Two-Part Inventions, Three-Part Sinfonias. 312pp. 8⅛ x 11. 0-486-22360-4

Bach, Johann Sebastian, ORGAN MUSIC. Bach-Gesellschaft edition. 93 works. 6 Trio Sonatas, German Organ Mass, Orgelbüchlein, Six Schubler Chorales, 18 Choral Preludes. 357pp. 8⅛ x 11. 0-486-22359-0

Bach, Johann Sebastian, TOCCATAS, FANTASIAS, PASSACAGLIA AND OTHER WORKS FOR ORGAN. Over 20 best-loved works including Toccata and Fugue in D Minor, BWV 565; Passacaglia and Fugue in C Minor, BWV 582, many more. Bach-Gesellschaft edition. 176pp. 9 x 12. 0-486-25403-8

Bach, Johann Sebastian, TWO- AND THREE-PART INVENTIONS. Reproduction of original autograph ms. Edited by Eric Simon. 62pp. 8⅛ x 11. 0-486-21982-8

Bach, Johann Sebastian, THE WELL-TEMPERED CLAVIER: Books I and II, Complete. All 48 preludes and fugues in all major and minor keys. Authoritative Bach-Gesellschaft edition. Explanation of ornaments in English, tempo indications, music corrections. 208pp. 9⅜ x 12¼. 0-486-24532-2

Bartók, Béla, PIANO MUSIC OF BÉLA BARTÓK, Series I. New, definitive Archive Edition incorporating composer's corrections. Includes *Funeral March* from *Kossuth, Fourteen Bagatelles,* Bartók's break to modernism. 167pp. 9 x 12. (Available in U.S. only) 0-486-24108-4

Bartók, Béla, PIANO MUSIC OF BÉLA BARTÓK, Series II. Second in the Archive Edition incorporating composer's corrections. 85 short pieces *For Children, Two Elegies, Two Romanian Dances,* etc. 192pp. 9 x 12. (Available in U.S. only) 0-486-24109-2

Beethoven, Ludwig van, BAGATELLES, RONDOS AND OTHER SHORTER WORKS FOR PIANO. Most popular and most performed shorter works, including Rondo a capriccio in G and Andante in F. Breitkopf & Härtel edition. 128pp. 9⅜ x 12¼. 0-486-25392-9

Beethoven, Ludwig van, COMPLETE PIANO SONATAS. All sonatas in fine Schenker edition, with fingering, analytical material. One of best modern editions. 615pp. 9 x 12. Two-vol. set. 0-486-23134-8, 0-486-23135-6

Beethoven, Ludwig van, COMPLETE VARIATIONS FOR SOLO PIANO, Ludwig van Beethoven. Contains all 21 sets of Beethoven's piano variations, including the extremely popular *Diabelli Variations, Op. 120.* 240pp. 9⅜ x 12¼. 0-486-25188-8

Beethoven, Ludwig van, BEETHOVEN MASTERPIECES FOR SOLO PIANO: 25 Works. Twenty-five popular pieces include the Sonata in C-sharp Minor, Op. 27, No. 2 ("Moonlight"); Sonata in D Minor, Op. 31, No. 2 ("Tempest"); 32 Variations in C Minor; Andante in F Major; Rondo Capriccio, Op. 129; Fantasia, Op. 77; and popular bagatelles, rondos, minuets, and other works. 160pp. 9 x 12. 0-486-43570-9

Blesh, Rudi (ed.), CLASSIC PIANO RAGS. Best ragtime music (1897–1922) by Scott Joplin, James Scott, Joseph F. Lamb, Tom Turpin, nine others. 364pp. 9 x 12. Introduction by Blesh. 0-486-20469-3

Brahms, Johannes, COMPLETE SHORTER WORKS FOR SOLO PIANO. All solo music not in other two volumes. Waltzes, Scherzo in E Flat Minor, Eight Pieces, Rhapsodies, Fantasies, Intermezzi, etc. Vienna Gesellschaft der Musikfreunde. 180pp. 9 x 12. 0-486-22651-4

Brahms, Johannes, COMPLETE SONATAS AND VARIATIONS FOR SOLO PIANO. All sonatas, five variations on themes from Schumann, Paganini, Handel, etc. Vienna Gesellschaft der Musikfreunde edition. 178pp. 9 x 12. 0-486-22650-6

Brahms, Johannes, COMPLETE TRANSCRIPTIONS, CADENZAS AND EXERCISES FOR SOLO PIANO. Vienna Gesellschaft der Musikfreunde edition, vol. 15. Studies after Chopin, Weber, Bach; gigues, sarabandes; 10 Hungarian dances, etc. 178pp. 9 x 12. 0-486-22652-2

Byrd, William, MY LADY NEVELLS BOOKE OF VIRGINAL MUSIC. 42 compositions in modern notation from 1591 ms. For any keyboard instrument. 245pp. 8⅛ x 11. 0-486-22246-2

Chopin, Frédéric, COMPLETE BALLADES, IMPROMPTUS AND SONATAS. The four Ballades, four Impromptus and three Sonatas. Authoritative Mikuli edition. 192pp. 9 x 12. 0-486-24164-5

Chopin, Frédéric, COMPLETE MAZURKAS, Frédéric Chopin. 51 best-loved compositions, reproduced directly from the authoritative Kistner edition edited by Carl Mikuli. 160pp. 9 x 12. 0-486-25548-4

Chopin, Frédéric, COMPLETE PRELUDES AND ETUDES FOR SOLO PIANO. All 25 Preludes and all 27 Etudes by greatest piano music composer. Authoritative Mikuli edition. 192pp. 9 x 12. 0-486-24052-5

Chopin, Frédéric, FANTASY IN F MINOR, BARCAROLLE, BERCEUSE AND OTHER WORKS FOR SOLO PIANO. 15 works, including one of the greatest of the Romantic period, the Fantasy in F Minor, Op. 49, reprinted from the authoritative German edition prepared by Chopin's student, Carl Mikuli. 224pp. 8⅜ x 11¼. 0-486-25950-1

Chopin, Frédéric, CHOPIN MASTERPIECES FOR SOLO PIANO: 46 Works. Includes Ballade No. 1 in G Minor, Berceuse, 3 ecossaises, 5 etudes, Fantaisie-Impromptu, Marche Funèbre, 8 mazurkas, 7 nocturnes, 3 polonaises, 9 preludes, Scherzo No. 2 in B-flat Minor, and 6 waltzes. Authoritative sources. 224pp. 9 x 12. 0-486-40150-2

Chopin, Frédéric, NOCTURNES AND POLONAISES. 20 *Nocturnes* and 11 *Polonaises* reproduced from the authoritative Mikuli edition for pianists, students, and musicologists. Commentary. 224pp. 9 x 12. 0-486-24564-0

Chopin, Frédéric, WALTZES AND SCHERZOS. All of the Scherzos and nearly all (20) of the Waltzes from the authoritative Mikuli edition. Editorial commentary. 160pp. 9 x 12. 0-486-24316-8

Cofone, Charles J. F. (ed.), ELIZABETH ROGERS HIR VIRGINALL BOOKE. All 112 pieces from noted 1656 manuscript, most never before published. Composers include Thomas Brewer, William Byrd, Orlando Gibbons, etc. Calligraphy by editor. 125pp. 9 x 12. 0-486-23138-0

Dover Piano and Keyboard Editions

Couperin, François, KEYBOARD WORKS/Series One: Ordres I–XIII; Series Two: Ordres XIV–XXVII and Miscellaneous Pieces. Over 200 pieces. Reproduced directly from edition prepared by Johannes Brahms and Friedrich Chrysander. Total of 496pp. 8⅛ x 11.
Series I: 0-486-25795-9; Series II: 0-486-25796-7

Debussy, Claude, COMPLETE PRELUDES, Books 1 and 2. 24 evocative works that reveal the essence of Debussy's genius for musical imagery, among them many of the composer's most famous piano compositions. Glossary of French terms. 128pp. 8⅜ x 11¼.
0-486-25970-6

Debussy, Claude, DEBUSSY MASTERPIECES FOR SOLO PIANO: 20 Works. From France's most innovative and influential composer—a rich compilation of works that include "Golliwogg's cakewalk," "Engulfed cathedral," "Clair de lune," and 17 others. 128pp. 9 x 12. 0-486-42425-1

Debussy, Claude, PIANO MUSIC 1888–1905. Deux Arabesques, Suite Bergamasque, Masques, first series of Images, etc. Nine others, in corrected editions. 175pp. 9⅜ x 12¼.
0-486-22771-5

Dvořák, Antonín, HUMORESQUES AND OTHER WORKS FOR SOLO PIANO. Humoresques, Op. 101, complete, Silhouettes, Op. 8, Poetic Tone Pictures, Theme with Variations, Op. 36, 4 Slavonic Dances, more. 160pp. 9 x 12.
0-486-28355-0

de Falla, Manuel, AMOR BRUJO AND EL SOMBRERO DE TRES PICOS FOR SOLO PIANO. With these two popular ballets, El Amor Brujo (Love, the Magician) and El Sombrero de Tres Picos (The Three-Cornered Hat), Falla brought the world's attention to the music of Spain. The composer himself made these arrangements of the complete ballets for piano solo. xii+132pp. 9 x 12.
0-486-44170-9

Fauré, Gabriel, COMPLETE PRELUDES, IMPROMPTUS AND VALSES-CAPRICES. Eighteen elegantly wrought piano works in authoritative editions. Only one-volume collection available. 144pp. 9 x 12. (Not available in France or Germany)
0-486-25789-4

Fauré, Gabriel, NOCTURNES AND BARCAROLLES FOR SOLO PIANO. 12 nocturnes and 12 barcarolles reprinted from authoritative French editions. 208pp. 9⅜ x 12¼. (Not available in France or Germany)
0-486-27955-3

Feofanov, Dmitry (ed.), RARE MASTERPIECES OF RUSSIAN PIANO MUSIC: Eleven Pieces by Glinka, Balakirev, Glazunov and Others. Glinka's *Prayer*, Balakirev's *Reverie*, Liapunov's *Transcendental Etude, Op. 11, No. 10,* and eight others—full, authoritative scores from Russian texts. 144pp. 9 x 12.
0-486-24659-0

Franck, César, ORGAN WORKS. Composer's best-known works for organ, including Six Pieces, Trois Pieces, and Trois Chorals. Oblong format for easy use at keyboard. Authoritative Durand edition. 208pp. 11⅜ x 8¼.
0-486-25517-4

Gottschalk, Louis M., PIANO MUSIC. 26 pieces (including covers) by early 19th-century American genius. "Bamboula," "The Banjo," other Creole, Negro-based material, through elegant salon music. 301pp. 9¼ x 12.
0-486-21683-7

Granados, Enrique, GOYESCAS, SPANISH DANCES AND OTHER WORKS FOR SOLO PIANO. Great Spanish composer's most admired, most performed suites for the piano, in definitive Spanish editions. 176pp. 9 x 12.
0-486-25481-X

Grieg, Edvard, COMPLETE LYRIC PIECES FOR PIANO. All 66 pieces from Grieg's ten sets of little mood pictures for piano, favorites of generations of pianists. 224pp. 9⅜ x 12¼.
0-486-26176-X

Handel, G. F., KEYBOARD WORKS FOR SOLO INSTRUMENTS. 35 neglected works from Handel's vast oeuvre, originally jotted down as improvisations. Includes Eight Great Suites, others. New sequence. 174pp. 9⅜ x 12¼.
0-486-24338-9

Haydn, Joseph, COMPLETE PIANO SONATAS. 52 sonatas reprinted from authoritative Breitkopf & Härtel edition. Extremely clear and readable; ample space for notes, analysis. 464pp. 9⅜ x 12¼.
Vol. I: 0-486-24726-0; Vol. II: 0-486-24727-9

Jasen, David A. (ed.), RAGTIME GEMS: Original Sheet Music for 25 Ragtime Classics. Includes original sheet music and covers for 25 rags, including three of Scott Joplin's finest: "Searchlight Rag," "Rose Leaf Rag," and "Fig Leaf Rag." 122pp. 9 x 12.
0-486-25248-5

Joplin, Scott, COMPLETE PIANO RAGS. All 38 piano rags by the acknowledged master of the form, reprinted from the publisher's original editions complete with sheet music covers. Introduction by David A. Jasen. 208pp. 9 x 12.
0-486-25807-6

Liszt, Franz, ANNÉES DE PÈLERINAGE, COMPLETE. Authoritative Russian edition of piano masterpieces: *Première Année (Suisse): Deuxième Année (Italie)* and *Venezia e Napoli; Troisième Année,* other related pieces. 288pp. 9⅜ x 12¼.
0-486-25627-8

Liszt, Franz, BEETHOVEN SYMPHONIES NOS. 6–9 TRANSCRIBED FOR SOLO PIANO. Includes Symphony No. 6 in F major, Op. 68, "Pastorale"; Symphony No. 7 in A major, Op. 92; Symphony No. 8 in F major, Op. 93; and Symphony No. 9 in D minor, Op. 125, "Choral." A memorable tribute from one musical genius to another. 224pp. 9 x 12. 0-486-41884-7

Liszt, Franz, COMPLETE ETUDES FOR SOLO PIANO, Series I: Including the Transcendental Etudes, edited by Busoni. Also includes Etude in 12 Exercises, 12 Grandes Etudes and Mazeppa. Breitkopf & Härtel edition. 272pp. 8⅜ x 11¼.
0-486-25815-7

Liszt, Franz, COMPLETE ETUDES FOR SOLO PIANO, Series II: Including the Paganini Etudes and Concert Etudes, edited by Busoni. Also includes Morceau de Salon, Ab Irato. Breitkopf & Härtel edition. 192pp. 8⅜ x 11¼.
0-486-25816-5

Liszt, Franz, COMPLETE HUNGARIAN RHAPSODIES FOR SOLO PIANO. All 19 Rhapsodies reproduced directly from authoritative Russian edition. All headings, footnotes translated to English. 224pp. 8⅜ x 11¼.
0-486-24744-9

Liszt, Franz, LISZT MASTERPIECES FOR SOLO PIANO: 13 Works. Masterworks by the supreme piano virtuoso of the 19th century: *Hungarian Rhapsody No. 2 in C-sharp minor, Consolation No. 3 in D-Flat major, Liebestraum No. 3 in A-flat major, La Campanella* (Paganini Etude No. 3), and nine others. 128pp. 9 x 12.
0-486-41379-9

Liszt, Franz, MEPHISTO WALTZ AND OTHER WORKS FOR SOLO PIANO. Rapsodie Espagnole, Liebesträume Nos. 1–3, Valse Oubliée No. 1, Nuages Gris, Polonaises Nos. 1 and 2, Grand Galop Chromatique, more. 192pp. 8⅜ x 11¼.
0-486-28147-7

Liszt, Franz, PIANO TRANSCRIPTIONS FROM FRENCH AND ITALIAN OPERAS. Virtuoso transformations of themes by Mozart, Verdi, Bellini, other masters, into unforgettable music for piano. Published in association with American Liszt Society. 247pp. 9 x 12. 0-486-24273-0

Maitland, J. Fuller, Squire, W. B. (eds.), THE FITZWILLIAM VIRGINAL BOOK. Famous early 17th-century collection of keyboard music, 300 works by Morley, Byrd, Bull, Gibbons, etc. Modern notation. Total of 938pp. 8⅜ x 11. Two-vol. set.
0-486-21068-5, 0-486-21069-3

Medtner, Nikolai, COMPLETE FAIRY TALES FOR SOLO PIANO. Thirty-eight complex, surprising pieces by an underrated Russian 20th-century Romantic whose music is more cerebral and harmonically adventurous than Rachmaninoff's. 272pp. 9 x 12. (Available in U.S. only)
0-486-41683-6

Dover Piano and Keyboard Editions

Mendelssohn, Felix, COMPLETE WORKS FOR PIANOFORTE SOLO. Breitkopf and Härtel edition of Capriccio in F# Minor, Sonata in E Major, Fantasy in F# Minor, Three Caprices, Songs without Words, and 20 other works. Total of 416pp. 9⅜ x 12¼. Two-vol. set. 0-486-23136-4, 0-486-23137-2

Mozart, Wolfgang Amadeus, MOZART MASTERPIECES: 19 WORKS FOR SOLO PIANO. Superb assortment includes sonatas, fantasies, variations, rondos, minuets, and more. Highlights include "Turkish Rondo," "Sonata in C," and a dozen variations on "Ah, vous dirai-je, Maman" (the familiar tune "Twinkle, Twinkle, Little Star"). Convenient, attractive, inexpensive volume; authoritative sources. 128pp. 9 x 12. 0-486-40408-0

Pachelbel, Johann, THE FUGUES ON THE MAGNIFICAT FOR ORGAN OR KEYBOARD. 94 pieces representative of Pachelbel's magnificent contribution to keyboard composition; can be played on the organ, harpsichord or piano. 100pp. 9 x 12. (Available in U.S. only) 0-486-25037-7

Phillipp, Isidor (ed.), FRENCH PIANO MUSIC, AN ANTHOLOGY. 44 complete works, 1670–1905, by Lully, Couperin, Rameau, Alkan, Saint-Saëns, Delibes, Bizet, Godard, many others; favorite and lesser-known examples, all top quality. 188pp. 9 x 12. (Not available in France or Germany) 0-486-23381-2

Prokofiev, Sergei, PIANO SONATAS NOS. 1–4, OPP. 1, 14, 28, 29. Includes the dramatic Sonata No. 1 in F minor; Sonata No. 2 in D minor, a masterpiece in four movements; Sonata No. 3 in A minor, a brilliant 7-minute score; and Sonata No. 4 in C minor, a three-movement sonata considered vintage Prokofiev. 96pp. 9 x 12. (Available in U.S. only) 0-486-42128-7

Rachmaninoff, Serge, COMPLETE PRELUDES AND ETUDES-TABLEAUX. Forty-one of his greatest works for solo piano, including the riveting C Minor, G Minor and B Minor preludes, in authoritative editions. 208pp. 8⅝ x 11¼. 0-486-25696-0

Ravel, Maurice, PIANO MASTERPIECES OF MAURICE RAVEL. Handsome affordable treasury; *Pavane pour une infante defunte, jeux d'eau, Sonatine, Miroirs,* more. 128pp. 9 x 12. (Not available in France or Germany) 0-486-25137-3

Satie, Erik, GYMNOPÉDIES, GNOSSIENNES AND OTHER WORKS FOR PIANO. The largest Satie collection of piano works yet published, 17 in all, reprinted from the original French editions. 176pp. 9 x 12. (Not available in France or Germany) 0-486-25978-1

Satie, Erik, TWENTY SHORT PIECES FOR PIANO (Sports et Divertissements). French master's brilliant thumbnail sketches—verbal and musical—of various outdoor sports and amusements. English translations, 20 illustrations. Rare, limited 1925 edition. 48pp. 12 x 8¼. (Not available in France or Germany) 0-486-24365-6

Scarlatti, Domenico, GREAT KEYBOARD SONATAS, Series I and Series II. 78 of the most popular sonatas reproduced from the G. Ricordi edition edited by Alessandro Longo. Total of 320pp. 8⅝ x 11¼. Series I: 0-486-24996-4; Series II: 0-486-25003-2

Schubert, Franz, COMPLETE SONATAS FOR PIANOFORTE SOLO. All 15 sonatas. Breitkopf and Härtel edition. 293pp. 9⅜ x 12¼. 0-486-22647-6

Schubert, Franz, DANCES FOR SOLO PIANO. Over 350 waltzes, minuets, landler, ecossaises, and other charming, melodic dance compositions reprinted from the authoritative Breitkopf & Härtel edition. 192pp. 9⅜ x 12¼. 0-486-26107-7

Schubert, Franz, FIVE FAVORITE PIANO SONATAS. Here in one convenient, affordable volume are five great sonatas, including his last three, among the finest works ever composed for piano: *Sonata in C Minor, D. 958, A Major, D. 959,* and *B-flat Major, D. 960.* Also included are the sonatas in *A Minor, D. 784,* and *A Major, D. 664.* vi+122pp. 9 x 12. 0-486-44141-5

Schubert, Franz, SELECTED PIANO WORKS FOR FOUR HANDS. 24 separate pieces (16 most popular titles): Three Military Marches, Lebensstürme, Four Polonaises, Four Ländler, etc. Rehearsal numbers added. 273pp. 9 x 12. 0-486-23529-7

Schubert, Franz, SHORTER WORKS FOR PIANOFORTE SOLO. All piano music except Sonatas, Dances, and a few unfinished pieces. Contains Wanderer, Impromptus, Moments Musicals, Variations, Scherzi, etc. Breitkopf and Härtel edition. 199pp. 9⅜ x 12¼. 0-486-22648-4

Schumann, Clara (ed.), PIANO MUSIC OF ROBERT SCHUMANN, Series I. Major compositions from the period 1830–39; *Papillons,* Toccata, Grosse Sonate No. 1, *Phantasiestücke, Arabeske, Blumenstück,* and nine other works. Reprinted from Breitkopf & Härtel edition. 274pp. 9⅜ x 12¼. 0-486-21459-1

Schumann, Clara (ed.), PIANO MUSIC OF ROBERT SCHUMANN, Series II. Major compositions from period 1838–53; *Humoreske, Novelletten,* Sonate No. 2, 43 *Clavierstücke für die Jugend,* and six other works. Reprinted from Breitkopf & Härtel edition. 272pp. 9⅜ x 12¼. 0-486-21461-3

Schumann, Clara (ed.), PIANO MUSIC OF ROBERT SCHUMANN, Series III. All solo music not in other two volumes, including *Symphonic Etudes, Phantaisie,* 13 other choice works. Definitive Breitkopf & Härtel edition. 224pp. 9⅜ x 12¼. 0-486-23906-3

Scriabin, Alexander, COMPLETE PIANO SONATAS. All ten of Scriabin's sonatas, reprinted from an authoritative early Russian edition. 256pp. 8⅝ x 11¼. 0-486-25850-5

Scriabin, Alexander, THE COMPLETE PRELUDES AND ETUDES FOR PIANOFORTE SOLO. All the preludes and etudes including many perfectly spun miniatures. Edited by K. N. Igumnov and Y. I. Mil'shteyn. 250pp. 9 x 12. 0-486-22919-X

Sousa, John Philip, SOUSA'S GREAT MARCHES IN PIANO TRANSCRIPTION. Playing edition includes: "The Stars and Stripes Forever," "King Cotton," "Washington Post," much more. 24 illustrations. 111pp. 9 x 12. 0-486-23132-1

Strauss, Johann, Jr., FAVORITE WALTZES, POLKAS AND OTHER DANCES FOR SOLO PIANO. "Blue Danube," "Tales from Vienna Woods," and many other best-known waltzes and other dances. 160pp. 9 x 12. 0-486-27851-4

Sweelinck, Jan Pieterszoon, WORKS FOR ORGAN AND KEYBOARD. Nearly all of early Dutch composer's difficult-to-find keyboard works. Chorale variations; toccatas, fantasias; variations on secular, dance tunes. Also, incomplete and/or modified works, plus fantasia by John Bull. 272pp. 9 x 12. 0-486-24935-2

Telemann, Georg Philipp, THE 36 FANTASIAS FOR KEYBOARD. Graceful compositions by 18th-century master. 1923 Breslauer edition. 80pp. 8⅛ x 11. 0-486-25365-1

Tichenor, Trebor Jay, (ed.), RAGTIME RARITIES. 63 tuneful, rediscovered piano rags by 51 composers (or teams). Does not duplicate selections in *Classic Piano Rags* (Dover, 20469-3). 305pp. 9 x 12. 0-486-23157-7

Tichenor, Trebor Jay, (ed.), RAGTIME REDISCOVERIES. 64 unusual rags demonstrate diversity of style, local tradition. Original sheet music. 320pp. 9 x 12. 0-486-23776-1

*Available from your music dealer or write for **free** Music Catalog to Dover Publications, Inc., Dept. MUBI, 31 East 2nd Street, Mineola, NY 11501*
*Visit us online at **www.doverpublications.com***

Dover Opera, Choral and Lieder Scores

Bach, Johann Sebastian, EASTER ORATORIO IN FULL SCORE. Reproduces the authoritative Bach-Gesellschaft edition, in which the vocal parts of the third version of the oratorio were collated with the score of the first revision in an attempt to discover Bach's final intentions. Instrumentation. New English translation of text. 80pp. 9 x 12. 0-486-41890-1

Bach, Johann Sebastian, ELEVEN GREAT CANTATAS. Full vocal-instrumental score from Bach-Gesellschaft edition. *Christ lag in Todesbanden, Ich hatte viel Bekümmerniss, Jauchhzet Gott in allen Landen,* eight others. Study score. 350pp. 9 x 12. 0-486-23268-9

Bach, Johann Sebastian, MASS IN B MINOR IN FULL SCORE. The crowning glory of Bach's lifework in the field of sacred music and a universal statement of Christian faith, reprinted from the authoritative Bach-Gesellschaft edition. Translation of texts. 320pp. 9 x 12. 0-486-25992-7

Bach, Johann Sebastian, SEVEN GREAT SACRED CANTATAS IN FULL SCORE. Seven favorite sacred cantatas. Printed from a clear, modern engraving and sturdily bound; new literal line-for-line translations. Reliable Bach-Gesellschaft edition. Complete German texts. 256pp. 9 x 12. 0-486-24950-6

Bach, Johann Sebastian, SIX GREAT SECULAR CANTATAS IN FULL SCORE. Bach's nearest approach to comic opera. *Hunting Cantata, Wedding Cantata, Aeolus Appeased, Phoebus and Pan, Coffee Cantata,* and *Peasant Cantata.* 286pp. 9 x 12. 0-486-23934-9

Beethoven, Ludwig van, FIDELIO IN FULL SCORE. Beethoven's only opera, complete in one affordable volume, including all spoken German dialogue. Republication of C. F. Peters, Leipzig edition. 272pp. 9 x 12. 0-486-24740-6

Bizet, Georges, CARMEN IN FULL SCORE. Complete, authoritative score of perhaps the world's most popular opera, in the version most commonly performed today, with recitatives by Ernest Guiraud. 574pp. 9 x 12. 0-486-25820-3

Brahms, Johannes, COMPLETE SONGS FOR SOLO VOICE AND PIANO (two volumes). A total of 113 songs in complete score by greatest lieder writer since Schubert. Series I contains 15-song cycle *Die Schone Magelone;* Series II includes famous "Lullaby." Total of 448pp. 9⅜ x 12¼. Series I: 0-486-23820-2; Series II: 0-486-23821-0

Brahms, Johannes, COMPLETE SONGS FOR SOLO VOICE AND PIANO: Series III. 64 songs, published from 1877 to 1886, include such favorites as "Geheimnis," "Alte Liebe," and "Vergebliches Standchen." 224pp. 9 x 12. 0-486-23822-9

Brahms, Johannes, COMPLETE SONGS FOR SOLO VOICE AND PIANO: Series IV. 120 songs that complete the Brahms song oeuvre, with sensitive arrangements of 91 folk and traditional songs. 240pp. 9 x 12. 0-486-23823-7

Brahms, Johannes, GERMAN REQUIEM IN FULL SCORE. Definitive Breitkopf & Härtel edition of Brahms's greatest vocal work, fully scored for solo voices, mixed chorus and orchestra. 208pp. 9⅜ x 12¼. 0-486-25486-0

Debussy, Claude, PELLÉAS ET MÉLISANDE IN FULL SCORE. Reprinted from the E. Fromont (1904) edition, this volume faithfully reproduces the full orchestral-vocal score of Debussy's sole and enduring opera masterpiece. 416pp. 9 x 12. (Available in U.S. only) 0-486-24825-9

Debussy, Claude, SONGS, 1880–1904. Rich selection of 36 songs set to texts by Verlaine, Baudelaire, Pierre Louÿs, Charles d'Orleans, others. 175pp. 9 x 12. 0-486-24131-9

Fauré, Gabriel, SIXTY SONGS. "Clair de lune," "Apres un reve," "Chanson du pecheur," "Automne," and other great songs set for medium voice. Reprinted from French editions. 288pp. 8⅜ x 11. (Not available in France or Germany) 0-486-26534-X

Gilbert, W. S. and Sullivan, Sir Arthur, THE AUTHENTIC GILBERT & SULLIVAN SONGBOOK, 92 songs, uncut, original keys, in piano renderings approved by Sullivan. 399pp. 9 x 12. 0-486-23482-7

Gilbert, W. S. and Sullivan, Sir Arthur, HMS PINAFORE IN FULL SCORE. New edition by Carl Simpson and Ephraim Hammett Jones. Some of Gilbert's most clever flashes of wit and a number of Sullivan's most charming melodies in a handsome, authoritative new edition based on original manuscripts and early sources. 256pp. 9 x 12. 0-486-42201-1

Gilbert, W. S. and Sullivan, Sir Arthur (Carl Simpson and Ephraim Hammett Jones, eds.), THE PIRATES OF PENZANCE IN FULL SCORE. New performing edition corrects numerous errors, offers performers the choice of two versions of the Act II finale, and gives the first accurate full score of the "Climbing over Rocky Mountain" section. 288pp. 9 x 12. 0-486-41891-X

Grieg, Edvard, FIFTY SONGS FOR HIGH VOICE. Outstanding compilation includes many of his most popular melodies, such as "Solvejg's Song," "From Monte Pincio," and "Dreams." Introduction. Notes. 176pp. 9 x 12. 0-486-44130-X

Hale, Philip (ed.), FRENCH ART SONGS OF THE NINETEENTH CENTURY: 39 Works from Berlioz to Debussy. 39 songs from romantic period by 18 composers: Berlioz, Chausson, Debussy (six songs), Gounod, Massenet, Thomas, etc. French text, English singing translation for high voice. 182pp. 9 x 12. (Not available in France or Germany) 0-486-23680-3

Handel, George Frideric, GIULIO CESARE IN FULL SCORE. Great Baroque masterpiece reproduced directly from authoritative Deutsche Handelgesellschaft edition. Gorgeous melodies, inspired orchestration. Complete and unabridged. 160pp. 9⅜ x 12¼. 0-486-25056-3

Handel, George Frideric, MESSIAH IN FULL SCORE. An authoritative full-score edition of the oratorio that is the best-known, most-beloved, most-performed large-scale musical work in the English-speaking world. 240pp. 9 x 12. 0-486-26067-4

Monteverdi, Claudio, MADRIGALS: BOOK IV & V. 39 finest madrigals with new line-for-line literal English translations of the poems facing the Italian text. 256pp. 8⅛ x 11. (Available in U.S. only) 0-486-25102-0

Mozart, Wolfgang Amadeus, THE ABDUCTION FROM THE SERAGLIO IN FULL SCORE. Mozart's early comic masterpiece, exactingly reproduced from the authoritative Breitkopf & Härtel edition. 320pp. 9 x 12. 0-486-26004-6

Mozart, Wolfgang Amadeus, COSI FAN TUTTE IN FULL SCORE. Scholarly edition of one of Mozart's greatest operas. Da Ponte libretto. Commentary. Preface. Translated Front Matter. 448pp. 9⅜ x 12¼. (Available in U.S. only) 0-486-24528-4

Mozart, Wolfgang Amadeus, DON GIOVANNI: COMPLETE ORCHESTRAL SCORE. Full score that contains everything from the original version, along with later arias, recitatives, and duets added to original score for Vienna performance. Peters edition. Study score. 468pp. 9⅜ x 12¼. (Available in U.S. only) 0-486-23026-0

Mozart, Wolfgang Amadeus, THE MAGIC FLUTE (DIE ZAUBERFLÖTE) IN FULL SCORE. Authoritative C. F. Peters edition of Mozart's brilliant last opera still widely popular. Includes all the spoken dialogue. 226pp. 9 x 12. 0-486-24783-X

Mozart, Wolfgang Amadeus, THE MARRIAGE OF FIGARO: COMPLETE SCORE. Finest comic opera ever written. Full score, beautifully engraved, includes passages often cut in other editions. Peters edition. Study score. 448pp. 9⅜ x 12¼. (Available in U.S. only) 0-486-23751-6

Available from your music dealer or write for free Music Catalog to
Dover Publications, Inc., Dept. MUBI, 31 East 2nd Street, Mineola, NY 11501
Visit us online at www.doverpublications.com

Dover Opera, Choral and Lieder Scores

Mozart, Wolfgang Amadeus, REQUIEM IN FULL SCORE. Masterpiece of vocal composition, among the most recorded and performed works in the repertoire. Authoritative edition published by Breitkopf & Härtel, Wiesbaden. 203pp. 8⅜ x 11¼. 0-486-25311-2

Offenbach, Jacques, OFFENBACH'S SONGS FROM THE GREAT OPERETTAS. Piano, vocal (French text) for 38 most popular songs: *Orphée, Belle Hélène, Vie Parisienne, Duchesse de Gérolstein,* others. 21 illustrations. 195pp. 9 x 12. 0-486-23341-3

Prokokiev, Sergei, THE LOVE FOR THREE ORANGES VOCAL SCORE. Surrealistic fairy tale satirizes traditional operatic forms with a daring and skillful combination of humor, sorrow, fantasy, and grotesquery. Russian and French texts. iv+252pp. 7½ x 10¾. (Available in the U.S. only.) 0-486-44169-5

Puccini, Giacomo, LA BOHÈME IN FULL SCORE. Authoritative Italian edition of one of the world's most beloved operas. English translations of list of characters and instruments. 416pp. 8⅜ x 11¼. (Not available in United Kingdom, France, Germany or Italy) 0-486-25477-1

Rachmaninoff, Serge, THE BELLS IN FULL SCORE. Written for large orchestra, solo vocalists, and chorus, loosely based on Poe's brilliant poem with added material from the Russian translation that permits Rachmaninoff to develop the themes in a more intense, dark idiom. x+118pp. 9⅜ x 12¼. 0-486-44149-0

Rossini, Gioacchino, THE BARBER OF SEVILLE IN FULL SCORE. One of the greatest comic operas ever written, reproduced here directly from the authoritative score published by Ricordi. 464pp. 8⅜ x 11¼. 0-486-26019-4

Schubert, Franz, COMPLETE SONG CYCLES. Complete piano, vocal music of *Die Schöne Müllerin, Die Winterreise, Schwanengesang.* Also Drinker English singing translations. Breitkopf & Härtel edition. 217pp. 9⅜ x 12¼. 0-486-22649-2

Schubert, Franz, SCHUBERT'S SONGS TO TEXTS BY GOETHE. Only one-volume edition of Schubert's Goethe songs from authoritative Breitkopf & Härtel edition, plus all revised versions. New prose translation of poems. 84 songs. 256pp. 9⅜ x 12¼. 0-486-23752-4

Schubert, Franz, 59 FAVORITE SONGS. "Der Wanderer," "Ave Maria," "Hark, Hark, the Lark," and 56 other masterpieces of lieder reproduced from the Breitkopf & Härtel edition. 256pp. 9⅜ x 12¼. 0-486-24849-6

Schumann, Robert, SELECTED SONGS FOR SOLO VOICE AND PIANO. Over 100 of Schumann's greatest lieder, set to poems by Heine, Goethe, Byron, others. Breitkopf & Härtel edition. 248pp. 9⅜ x 12¼. 0-486-24202-1

Strauss, Richard, DER ROSENKAVALIER IN FULL SCORE. First inexpensive edition of great operatic masterpiece, reprinted complete and unabridged from rare, limited Fürstner edition (1910) approved by Strauss. 528pp. 9⅜ x 12¼. (Available in U.S. only) 0-486-25498-4

Strauss, Richard, DER ROSENKAVALIER: VOCAL SCORE. Inexpensive edition reprinted directly from original Fürstner (1911) edition of vocal score. Verbal text, vocal line and piano "reduction." 448pp. 8⅜ x 11¼. (Not available in Europe or the United Kingdom) 0-486-25501-8

Strauss, Richard, SALOME IN FULL SCORE. Atmospheric color predominates in composer's first great operatic success. Definitive Fürstner score, now extremely rare. 352pp. 9⅜ x 12¼. (Available in U.S. only) 0-486-24208-0

Stravinsky, Igor, SONGS 1906–1920. Brilliant interpretations of Russian folk songs collected for the first time in a single affordable volume. All scores are for voice and piano, with instrumental ensemble accompaniments to "Three Japanese Lyrics," "Pribaoutki," and "Berceuses du Chat" in full score as well as piano reduction. xiv+144pp. 9 x 12. 0-486-43821-X

Verdi, Giuseppe, AÏDA IN FULL SCORE. Verdi's glorious, most popular opera, reprinted from an authoritative edition published by G. Ricordi, Milan. 448pp. 9 x 12. 0-486-26172-7

Verdi, Giuseppe, FALSTAFF. Verdi's last great work, his first and only comedy. Complete unabridged score from original Ricordi edition. 480pp. 8⅜ x 11¼. 0-486-24017-7

Verdi, Giuseppe, OTELLO IN FULL SCORE. The penultimate Verdi opera, his tragic masterpiece. Complete unabridged score from authoritative Ricordi edition, with Front Matter translated. 576pp. 8¼ x 11. 0-486-25040-7

Verdi, Giuseppe, REQUIEM IN FULL SCORE. Immensely popular with choral groups and music lovers. Republication of edition published by C. F. Peters, Leipzig. Study score. 204pp. 9⅜ x 12¼. (Available in U.S. only) 0-486-23682-X

Wagner, Richard, DAS RHEINGOLD IN FULL SCORE. Complete score, clearly reproduced from B. Schott's authoritative edition. New translation of German Front Matter. 328pp. 9 x 12. 0-486-24925-5

Wagner, Richard, DIE MEISTERSINGER VON NÜRNBERG. Landmark in history of opera, in complete vocal and orchestral score of one of the greatest comic operas. C. F. Peters edition, Leipzig. Study score. 823pp. 8⅛ x 11. 0-486-23276-X

Wagner, Richard, DIE WALKÜRE. Complete orchestral score of the most popular of the operas in the Ring Cycle. Reprint of the edition published in Leipzig by C. F. Peters, ca. 1910. Study score. 710pp. 8⅜ x 11¼. 0-486-23566-1

Wagner, Richard, THE FLYING DUTCHMAN IN FULL SCORE. Great early masterpiece reproduced directly from limited Weingartner edition (1896), incorporating Wagner's revisions. Text, stage directions in English, German, Italian. 432pp. 9⅜ x 12¼. 0-486-25629-4

Wagner, Richard, GÖTTERDÄMMERUNG. Full operatic score, first time available in U.S. Reprinted directly from rare 1877 first edition. 615pp. 9⅜ x 12¼. 0-486-24250-1

Wagner, Richard, PARSIFAL IN FULL SCORE. Composer's deeply personal treatment of the legend of the Holy Grail, renowned for splendid music, glowing orchestration. C. F. Peters edition. 592pp. 8⅛ x 11. 0-486-25175-6

Wagner, Richard, SIEGFRIED IN FULL SCORE. *Siegfried,* third opera of Wagner's famous Ring Cycle, is reproduced from first edition (1876). 439pp. 9⅜ x 12¼. 0-486-24456-3

Wagner, Richard, TANNHAUSER IN FULL SCORE. Reproduces the original 1845 full orchestral and vocal score as slightly amended in 1847. Included is the ballet music for Act I written for the 1861 Paris production. 576pp. 8⅜ x 11¼. 0-486-24649-3

Wagner, Richard, TRISTAN UND ISOLDE. Full orchestral score with complete instrumentation. Study score. 655pp. 8⅛ x 11. 0-486-22915-7

von Weber, Carl Maria, DER FREISCHÜTZ. Full orchestral score to first Romantic opera, forerunner to Wagner and later developments. Still very popular. Study score, including full spoken text. 203pp. 9 x 12. 0-486-23449-5

Wolf, Hugo, THE COMPLETE MÖRIKE SONGS. Splendid settings to music of 53 German poems by Eduard Mörike, including "Der Tambour," "Elfenlied," and "Verborganheit." New prose translations. 208pp. 9⅜ x 12¼. 0-486-24380-X

Wolf, Hugo, SPANISH AND ITALIAN SONGBOOKS. Total of 90 songs by great 19th-century master of the genre. Reprint of authoritative C. F. Peters edition. New Translations of German texts. 256pp. 9⅜ x 12¼. 0-486-26156-5

*Available from your music dealer or write for **free** Music Catalog to*
Dover Publications, Inc., Dept. MUBI, 31 East 2nd Street, Mineola, NY 11501
*Visit us online at **www.doverpublications.com***